The Galaxy Global Eatery

Hemp Cookbook

The Galaxy Global Eatery
Hemp Cookbook

Denis Cicero

With Chefs Kris Czartoryski,
Suzanne Gruber, and Michael Lipp

Photographs by Michelle Hood

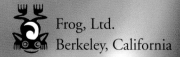

Frog, Ltd.
Berkeley, California

Published by Frog, Ltd.

Frog, Ltd. books are distributed by
North Atlantic Books
P.O. Box 12327
Berkeley, California 94712

Cover and book design by Paula Morrison

Printed in Singapore

The postcards printed throughout this book are reproduced courtesy of HempTrivia, manufacturer of postcards, posters, and notepads, www.hemptrivia.com.

North Atlantic Books' publications are available through most bookstores. For further information, call 800-337-2665 or visit our website at www.northatlanticbooks.com. Substantial discounts on bulk quantities are available to corporations, professional associations, and other organizations. For details and discount information, contact our special sales department.

Library of Congress Cataloging-in-Publication Data
Cicero, Denis.
        The galaxy global eatery hemp cookbook / by Denis Cicero.
              p. cm.
        Includes bibliographical references and index.
ISBN 1-58394-055-3
1. Cookery (Hemp) 2. Cookery, International. I. Title

    TX814.5.H45 C53 2001
    641.6'3—dc21
                                                        2001040633

 1 2 3 4 5 6 7 8 9 / 07 06 05 04 03 02

To Julia Butterfly Hill —

Modern American Hero

Only after the last tree has been cut down,
Only after the last River has been poisoned,
Only after the last fish has been caught,
Only then will you find that money cannot be eaten.
—*Cree Indian proverb*

Acknowledgements

Michelle Hood, my soulmate who brought me to North Atlantic Books. My partners Tom and Emmanuelle Hill, James McCaffrey, and Andrew Rasiej for giving me the opportunity to freely express myself. Chef Deborah Stanton for creatively sprouting the hempseed onto the plate. Chefs Michael Lipp, Susan Gruber, and Kris Czartoryski, my *jungle mate*, for carrying the baton. Don Wirtshafter for his leadership and pioneering efforts in hemp foods. Chris Conrad, John Roulac, Jack Herrer, Rowan Robinson, and Kenneth Jones, whose writings gave me the knowledge to teach others about this amazing seed. Lutz Amend of Hampf Dampf in Germany; and John Howell, who *set me free*. Paul Bastin, who *reeled* us to the press. *Papa* Al Finberg. My mother, Anita Rose, whose glass was always half full, and my brother Tom, whose spirit guides my love for nature. My twin sister, Didi, along with Mario, Larry, Jim, and Marjean for completing the circle; and Brooke Warner, my editor, for her patient guidance and perseverance in bringing the book to fruition.

Galaxy's Legendary Hall of Fame: Brendan Spiro, *Philosopher-Poet* and Manager Extraordinaire of the Galaxy Global Eatery; *Sexy* Naomi Barron—the best bartender in the universe; The A-Team: Amy Korb, Kristy Hinchcliffe, Sadie James, and Goldie Gareza; Linda Peng, Taylor Stanley, V, Ming, Tamara Grothaus, Andy Birss, Syam, Corrine, DJ Derek Jones, *Smooth* Brent, *Sweet* Megan, *Master Renaissance Man* Brian Olson, *Queen* Erin Sullivan, *Princess* Emy Hoexter, *Bad Boy* Brian Buckley, Chris Hasslebeck, *Boy* George McCormack, and Pumla and Leigh Anne for bringing South Africa to the Galaxy. Giselle, Pedro, *The Man*, for being the glue of the Galaxy; Sous Chef Michael Heran for his Mojo; Roger Connors, *The Rock*, who has seen me through the hard times with steadfastness and dedication. My *Guru* Alfred Nesarajah, who showed me the "Green"; Seyamack Kouretchian, *The Doctor*, who gave me structure and guidance through the legal maze; Michael Burisch, partner in HempSound.com, who brought Vienna to the Galaxy; Rick and Beth, the *Image Makers*; Los Jefes of the line: Antonio Martinez, Gamalliel, and Tolentino "Freddy" Alvarez, without whom there would be no Galaxy. The unsung heroes: Jose Luis, Eduardo, Ignacio, and Mark, the *King of Prep*. Tim Durette; Yogini Stephanie; Ian Brathwaite; and John McNamara for building my dream. Roberta, my first customer.

To all our loyal patrons and Hempsters worldwide for their undying support and loving energy.

And last but not least, all those who dedicate their thoughts and deeds to caring for Mother Earth.

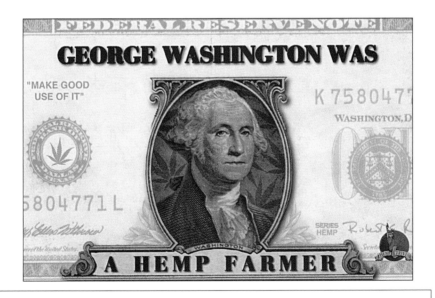

George Washington and Thomas Jefferson grew cannabis on their plantations.

GALAXY GLOBAL EATERY NYC
you can't eat money

LUMINI

Agave roasted Acorn squash ... $7.95
over apple cider braised greens

Hempnut Edamame Cakes ... $7.95
Boston bibb lettuce, spicy mango sauce

Cornmeal Crusted Tofu Steak ... $8.95
Iroquois jalapeno-agave succotash

BBQ Buffalo Seitan ... $8.95
jasmine rice, spinach, choclo & crispy Japanese eggplant

Seitan Enchilada ... $8.95
red and poblano peppers, black beans, mole, jalapeño rice

Indonesian Gado Gado ... $8.95
marinated cucumbers, carrots, Chinese long beans, tofu, hard boiled egg, peanut sauce, organic sunflower sprouts, cumin viniagrette

SPHEROIDS

Smoked Eel Burger ... $10.95
beet fries, cucumber seaweed salad, tonkatsu sauce

Blackened Tofu Sandwich ... $8.75
sautéed mushrooms, avocado, sun-dried tomatoes, spicy mango sauce

Hempnut Veggie Burger ... $8.75

Galaxy Burger ... $8.75

Turkey Burger ... $8.75

TBLT ... $7.95
turkey bacon, lettuce, tomato, bolo lavado

IONs

Edamame ... $5.95
fresh sea salted soybeans

Portuguese Caldo Verde ... $5.95
potato soup with kale served with spent beer grain broa

Mama Mojo's Platanos ... $6.95
chocolate banana and maize breads, spicy sautéed plantains, birdseye chili sals

Spicy Japanese Veget Pot Stickers ...
warm pum apple cider w

Korean Lettuce Wra
fresh water ch & spicy b

Chinese Taro Root
swe organic blac

Crispy C
spicy ric

LIVE

Organic B
her
or fig hem

Nut'n

Cucumbe
b
spro
organic sunfl
cumin

Chef K Czar in the SPECTRUM

Ask about our hemp products

printed on 100% tree-free hemp paper.

We do not accept personal or travelers check.

a 20% gratuity is added to parties of 6 or more.

$15 minimum on all credit cards.

Inquire about our catering menu for your next event.

www.galaxyglobaleatery.com
www.hempnut.com

Contents

The Galaxy Global Eatery Hemp Cookbook

The Big Bang

September 1995

After almost twenty years of tableside formal service in the restaurant industry, I hung up the tuxedo and suit for the last time. I was retiring from the business. I had dreams of travel, writing romance novels, and becoming a barefoot poet in San Francisco. No longer would I be subjected to the capricious needs of a demanding clientele or the two-hundred-bottle wine cellar! Who needs it? Food critics? Get a life. I'm going on the road....

"This business is smoke and mirrors!" I exclaimed. "I don't care how much money you spend designing a room, or who you hire to be your publicist! All you need is a VIBE and ONE unique ingredient that people remember. With the vibe you have their heart and soul. With the ingredient you have the pathway home—through their stomach."

"Give me a cardboard box and I'll give you a restaurant," I ranted to a friend and went traveling.

A month later, I picked up an email in Chiang Mai in Northern Thailand. It was from a dear friend and, unbeknownst to me, my future business partner.

"Hey Denis. Guess what? I have a cardboard box and I want you to give me a restaurant. And guess what else? Since you say that you don't need money, we are only giving you seventy-five thousand dollars to open, fully licensed and insured!"

And so the challenge began. Returning to New York, I visited the cardboard box. It was an old Greek diner located next to a rock-and-roll venue on Irving Place: one thousand square feet of bad Formica and crusty grease.

An old sign hanging on the side of the building read "Galaxy Restaurant."

"Well at least that leaves room for some interpretation," I surmised. "A mission statement from Mars perhaps—Innovative Foods for Progressive Palates."

"Sounds great," my friend proclaimed. "But what are you going to do in this dump that is innovative and progressive?"

"I'll get back to you," I said.

March 15, 1996
The Ides of March

After six months of hard labor, the "cardboard box" was now a cobalt blue and stainless interior with eleven hundred and twenty-five optic fibers in the ceiling enveloping hand blown glass fixtures and a magical sound system.

The restaurant was fully licensed and insured and had ninety dollars remaining in the bank. There was no proper ventilation, air conditioning, or heating system. My mother had passed away the week prior. I assembled the best staff New York had to offer and proceeded to explain the challenge. As I spoke, you could see my breath from the fifteen-degree weather outside.

"We will open this restaurant tonight regardless of the obstacles and will succeed based on two things—the VIBE and ONE special ingredient." (I still didn't know what that was going to be.)

We fired up the stoves, and blue smoke filled the room. The Galaxy looked like it was giving birth to Satan's son.

April 1996

You are only as good as the people you work with. I proved that over the winter of 1995–96. The new staff was full of hospitality and warmth, with a sense of humor that belied any of the nightmares we experienced together. Sexy, Hip, and Attentive all rolled up into one. In April of 1996 I was rummaging through some old papers and poems from 1978, when I lived on Martha's Vineyard working as cook in a small creperie. Lo and behold! The special ingredient was in a pancake recipe that I used to make for my bohemian friends. It was a cannabis seed. We called them cannacakes. Stashed next to the poems was a tiny cookbook entitled *The Hempseed Cookbook* by Carol Miller and Don Wirtshafter published years later, in 1991. It was as if I found the Holy Grail.

June 1996

Opening the twenty-five-pound pail of hempseed from Don Wirtshafter of the Ohio Hempery, I asked the chef to make a special for the night. "Do it with a sense of humor but take it seriously as a food ingredient," I asked of him. We prepared three dishes of clam bisque with hempseed and hemp oil—one for the chef, one for me, and one to sell for customer response. That customer, it turned out, was Eric Asimov from *The New York Times*. He reviewed us the next week and "The Galaxy" exploded into the Big Bang. And, as they say, "the rest is history." Hemp food was here to stay.

2001 Space Odyssey

For the next four years, The Galaxy Global Eatery revolutionized hemp cuisine, being recognized in most major culinary magazines, the TV Food Network, EXTRA, CNN, CNBC, and Charles Osgood's radio show. The mission statement was fulfilled, at least temporarily. In the acclaimed restaurant guide, *Zagats Survey*, we were reviewed favorably but the last line of the review asked, "What is Hemp"? Thus another mission was established, *The Galaxy Global Eatery Hemp Cookbook*.

The goal was to answer this question and to bring hempseed as a staple ingredient to the average person, across demographic lines, and help educate the masses as to the nutritional qualities of this forgotten seed. My hope is that we can move ONE person to use this incredible ingredient as a food source, high in protein, minerals, and essential fatty acids.

Hempseed has been utilized as a food source for thousands of years. The focus of this book is about NUTRITION and FOOD, not politics. We have selected a series of recipes that are meant to satisfy an array of culinary appetites.

The Galaxy Global Eatery encourages a low sodium, low dairy approach to dining, but realizes that the vast majority of people still like to use these ingredients. A diet high in fiber, fruit, and vegetables is also suggested, but we have included some poultry, fish, and meat items for those people who are interested in these types of recipes. I realize that we cannot be all things to all people, and as such, have chosen an interesting set of recipes to satisfy our readership.

There has been much discussion concerning THC (tetrahydracannabinol) in hemp foods. I personally don't want to engage this argument but feel it should be addressed. In the European Union and Canada, where hemp is legal, there are acceptable limits sanctioned by health institutes of various countries in the range of 0.3 percent THC.

As of October 9, 2001, in the United States, the Drug Enforcement Agency has published an interim ruling stating a zero tolerance for THC content in hemp foods. The Galaxy Global Eatery has tested its hemp foods with the Associated Analytical Laboratories in New York City in the past and has found nondetectable limits of THC. At the time of this writing, the hemp food industry is burgeoning and is well positioned to feed countless thousands of people in the world. In my lifetime I have not witness such interest in a new food source. In the aftermath of the World Trade Center bombings, you would think that our government agencies would find better ways to spend our tax dollars than attempting to squash new industries. Those of us who were down at Ground Zero fully appreciate that Food, Shelter, Love, and Compassion are concepts worthy of discussion. The rest of the argument I will leave up to the pundits and politicians. I don't know how this controversy will be resolved. I do know that if the God of all human beings places a seed, any seed, into Mother Earth that is capable of nourishing his children, I suspect he would frown on those who would take it from us.

God bless Mother Earth, and if we don't see you in The Galaxy, we hope you enjoy our recipes at home.

Denis Cicero

The Galaxy, with its thirty-two seats, has served more than half a million people in the last five years. We now have air conditioning, proper ventilation, and heat. Emails abound from around the world, from Reykjavik to New Delhi, asking when we are going to open in their cities. Not to worry. We are coming. The Galaxy Global Eatery will open in the San Francisco Bay Area and either Amsterdam or London in the year 2003. Then on to Tokyo and South America.

With every vision there is a road. We will find the right fork.

The Galaxy has its own line of hemp products including the Cosmonut bar, hempseed, hempnuts, hempseed oil, hempseed soaps and shampoo, and hemp clothing. We have manufactured the first hemp composite chopsticks, and we hope that future Galaxy establishments will include decorative building materials made from hemp stone and fabric.

For more information visit us on the web at galaxyglobaleatery.com, hempnut.com, galaxyhempnut.com, and hempstone.com.

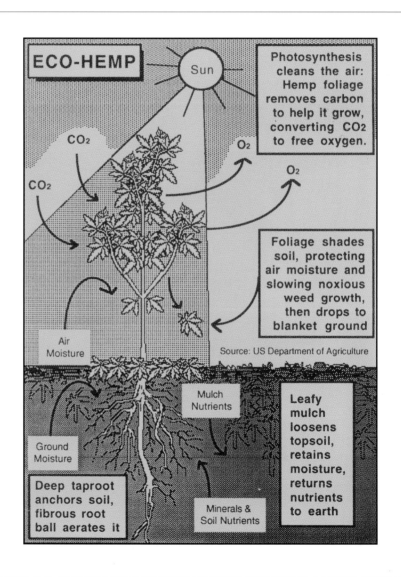

What Is Hemp?

Hemp is an annual herbaceous plant or crop that grows from seed. It is included in the botanical order Urticales, along with the hops plant (used to make beer), in a distinct family called Cannabaceae. Some botanists prefer to assign hemp to the Moraceae family, which includes the mulberry plant. The species is dioecious, meaning that it has two distinct sexes.

The flowers of hemp are highly developed, with the pollen-bearing staminate (male) flowers and the seed-producing pistillate (female) flowers blooming on separate plants. Some plants may be monoecious, or hermaphroditic.

Each part of the hemp plant has unique characteristics lending themselves to various beneficial applications. Its stalk envelops one of nature's longest and strongest soft fibers around a woody core containing close to 30 percent cellulose—the organic compound used in the manufacture of paper, plastics, film, and rayon, among others. Its leaves and roots build, aerate, and otherwise improve the soil by balancing the pH level and eliminating certain soil pathogens. Growing hemp can extract heavy-metal contaminants from chemically degraded farm land, reclaiming the land for organic food crop production. Hemp requires no pesticides, even when grown for industrial purposes on a large scale, and growing hemp can eliminate weeds without the use of herbicides. It can be fertilized using a combination of animal manure and rotation with nitrogen-fixing crops instead of chemical fertilizers. This makes it a wonderful crop for organic farming.

With its easy cultivation, rapid maturation cycle, and myriad of commercial applications for its fiber and oil, industrial hemp offers exceptional economic value to farmer and manufacturer alike. Currently there are at least twelve to fifteen different seed varietals grown for various applications, some of which are

cosmetic soaps and topical creams, animal bedding, paper production, biomass
fuel, paint varnishes, fabric for clothing, canvas for fine arts and nautical sails,
rope, as well as food.

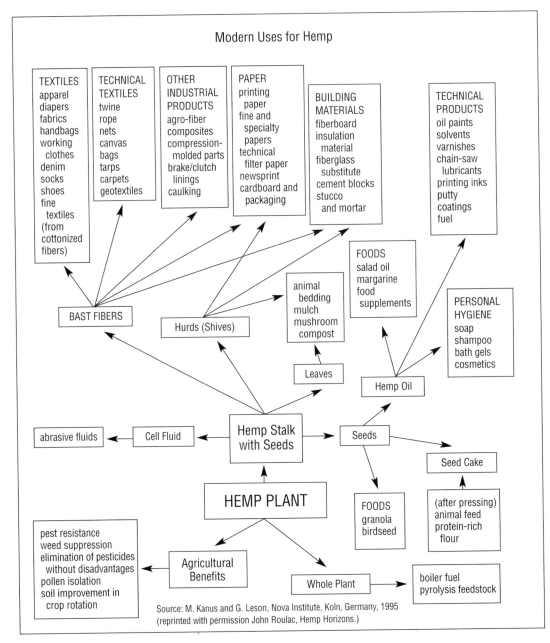

Modern Uses for Hemp

TEXTILES
apparel
diapers
fabrics
handbags
working
 clothes
denim
socks
shoes
fine
 textiles
(from
cottonized
fibers)

**TECHNICAL
TEXTILES**
twine
rope
nets
canvas
bags
tarps
carpets
geotextiles

**OTHER
INDUSTRIAL
PRODUCTS**
agro-fiber
composites
compression-
 molded parts
brake/clutch
 linings
caulking

PAPER
printing
 paper
fine and
 specialty
 papers
technical
 filter paper
newsprint
cardboard and
 packaging

**BUILDING
MATERIALS**
fiberboard
insulation
 material
fiberglass
 substitute
cement blocks
stucco
 and mortar

**TECHNICAL
PRODUCTS**
oil paints
solvents
varnishes
chain-saw
 lubricants
printing inks
putty
coatings
fuel

FOODS
salad oil
margarine
food
 supplements

**PERSONAL
HYGIENE**
soap
shampoo
bath gels
cosmetics

BAST FIBERS

Hurds (Shives)

animal
bedding
mulch
mushroom
compost

Leaves

Hemp Oil

abrasive fluids ← Cell Fluid ← Hemp Stalk
with Seeds → Seeds

Seed Cake

HEMP PLANT

FOODS
granola
birdseed

(after pressing)
animal feed
protein-rich
 flour

pest resistance
weed suppression
elimination of pesticides
 without disadvantages
pollen isolation
soil improvement in
 crop rotation

Agricultural
Benefits

Whole Plant

boiler fuel
pyrolysis feedstock

Source: M. Kanus and G. Leson, Nova Institute, Koln, Germany, 1995
(reprinted with permission John Roulac, Hemp Horizons.)

For the purposes of this book we will focus solely on the nutritional makeup of the seed, oil, nut, and flour to encourage the reader to include these tasty and healthy ingredients in their pantry at home.

The Hempseed

Botanically, hemp seeds are tiny nuts within shells or hulls that develop on the female flowers of the hemp plant. When they mature in late summer, they develop a thin, crunchy hull, gray or brownish in color with a marbled pattern. The seed hull protects the embryo, which consists of two pale seed leaves (the "nut" of the seed) and a tiny root. The hull contains mainly dietary fiber—carbohydrates that we can eat but not digest—and chlorophyll, which gives hemp oil its green color.

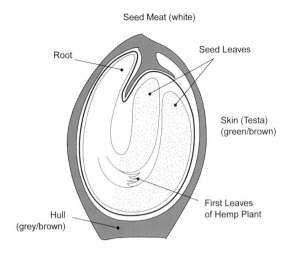

Seed Meat (white)

Root

Seed Leaves

Skin (Testa)
(green/brown)

First Leaves
of Hemp Plant

Hull
(grey/brown)

The nut represents the seed's center for energy storage and building materials. Proteins, small amounts of carbohydrates, and fat stored in tiny oil droplets in the cells make up most of the nut. Additional ingredients are found in smaller quantities: vitamins, phospholipids such as lecithin, phytosterols, and others.

Although seeds generally don't contain many vitamins, hempseed has a good quantity of the antioxidant vitamin E. It is also high in calcium, magnesium, phosphorus, potassium, and sulfur and low in heavy metals like strontium, thorium, arsenic, and chromium.

No other single plant source provides protein nutrition with all the essential amino acids in a favorable ratio for digestibility. Hempseeds contain approximately 25 percent protein. Hempseeds cannot serve as the sole source of protein, so it is wise to complement them with other protein sources such as fish, soy, or dairy. Some people are allergic to certain proteins in peanuts, soy, or whey, for example, but so far no allergies

Typical specifications for whole and shelled hempnuts and hempseed flour

	Hemp Oil
Fatty Acid Analysis*	
Saturated fatty acids	*in % of total fatty acids*
Palmitic acid (16:0)	6-9%
Stearic acid (18:0)	2-3.5%
Arachidic acid (20:0)	1-3%
Behenic acid (22:0)	<0.3%
Total saturated fatty acids	9-11%
Unsaturated fatty acids	*in % of total fatty acids*
Oleic acid (18:1 omega-9)	8.5-16%
Linoleic acid (18:2 omega-6)	53-60%
gamma-Linoleic acid GLA (18:3 omega-6)	1-4%
alpha-Linoleic acid (18:3 omega-3)	15-25%
Stearidonic acid (18:4 omega-3)	0.4-2%
Eicosaenoic acid (20:1)	<0.5%
Total unsaturated fatty acids	89-91%

Chemical Analysis

Vitamin E	100-150 mg/100g (mostly gamma tocopherol)
	13-20 IU/100g (as alpha-tocopherol equivalents)
Chlorophyll	50-20 ppm
THC Content	2-20 ppm
Specific Gravity	0.92 kg/1
Iodine value	155-170
Peroxide value	0.5-6.0 meq O_2/kg
Free Fatty Acids	0.5-2.0% as Oleic Acid
Phosphatides	100-400 ppm
Smoke Point	330° F (165° C)
Melting Point	18° F (-8° C)

Notes: * typical ranges for Central and Northern Europe varieties
1 ppm = 1 mg/kg

Source: adapted from Lan Chanvriere de L'Aube, Deferne & Pate 1996, nova-Institute 1998, Przybylski in Bioresource Hemp 1997, Wirtshafter in Bioresource Hemp 1995

to hempseed protein have been reported.

Whole hempseeds should be washed before use to clean any residual soil or broken seed pods. Simply place the seeds into a large container of water and let them soak. Dirt and cracked seeds will sink to the bottom and the good seeds will float. Remove and let drain in a colander before use. To toast the seeds, merely place them in a large skillet or wok on medium even heat and stir. Avoid overheating them or they will burn. Like popcorn, hempseeds are toasted when they begin to pop. Be careful not to burn them, as they will become bitter and turn black.

Hempseed Oil

*H*empseed oil contains all the essential fatty acids (EFAs) to maintain healthy human life. These acids are essential because the human body cannot produce them and so they must be obtained through the diet. EFAs are the raw materials for hormones, the body's communication network for cellular activity. Hempseed oil comprises 35 percent of the total seed weight and ranks among the lowest for saturated fatty acids at approximately 8 percent of total volume. This oil contains approximately 55 percent alphalinoleic acid (LA, also known as omega-6), 25 percent alpha-linolenic acid (LNA, also known as omega-3), and 2 percent gamma linolenic acid (GLA, also known as super omega-6). Only flax oil, also called linseed oil, has more linolenic acid at roughly 58 percent, but hempseed oil is the highest in total essential acids at 80 percent of total oil volume. Essential fatty acids are critical in all cell functions and body systems, and have proven effective in curbing and preventing many disease conditions such as eczema, psoriasis, cardiovascular disease, rheumatoid arthritis, osteoporosis, and premenstrual syndrome. In *Fat's that Heal, Fats that Kill,* author

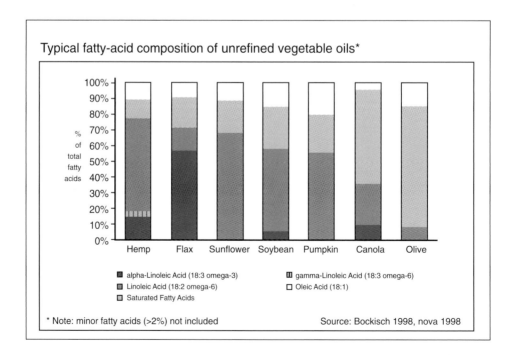

Typical fatty-acid composition of unrefined vegetable oils*

% of total fatty acids

Hemp, Flax, Sunflower, Soybean, Pumpkin, Canola, Olive

- alpha-Linoleic Acid (18:3 omega-3)
- Linoleic Acid (18:2 omega-6)
- Saturated Fatty Acids
- gamma-Linoleic Acid (18:3 omega-6)
- Oleic Acid (18:1)

* Note: minor fatty acids (>2%) not included

Source: Bockisch 1998, nova 1998

Eudo Erasmus states that because of the ideal ratio of essential fatty acids (3:1 of omega-6 to omega-3), hempseed oil may be nature's perfectly balanced oil.

Hempseed oil's high content of polyunsaturated fatty acids and its high omega-3:omega-6 ratio contribute to its nutritional value. These factors also cause instability and necessitate quality control throughout the production process since oil easily becomes rancid. Hempseed oil is generally cold-pressed in the absence of light for optimal color and flavor. Like other oils, the quality and taste of hempseed oil is determined by the manner in which different varieties of seed are grown, harvested, and handled. Oxygen, heat, and light are natural enemies of hempseed oil and careful attention should be placed in storing the oil. Rancidity occurs with exposure to these elements. Rancid oil is easily identified by unpleasant smell or taste ranging from bitter to buttery. Keep the oil in a dark glass or plastic bottle and refrigerate, or keep frozen when not in use. Shelf life should be at least six months if these precautions are heeded.

Finally, there has been much discussion concerning rancidity and sauté applications when cooking with hempseed oil. Though hemp cuisine is still being developed, we do know that the smoking point when heating hempseed oil is 320–330 degrees Fahrenheit or 165 degrees Centigrade. Tests have shown that high temperatures do not change the configuration of fatty acids in hempseed oil.

The Galaxy Global Eatery uses hempseed oil mostly as a truffle oil or for emulsifying in sauces and vinaigrettes. Low heat applications work as well with careful attention paid to the flash point of the oil.

Hempseed oil has a natural anti-inflammatory effect and helps to improve the condition of skin, hair, and nails.

Hempnuts

The greatest achievement in the burgeoning hemp food industry has been the technological "retooling" of seed dehulling machinery to extract the nut from the actual hempseed. The technology was first developed in 1996 by Franz Sieghl, managing director of "NOWAKORN," a cooperative of about eighty farmers in Austria who specialize in alternative grain production. The first hempnut for commercial use was delivered and marketed by Hanf Dampf in Esslingen, Germany, in August of 1997 and has since revolutionized the ability to utilize this wonderful food source. Since then, Jean Laprise

The author and Franz Sieghl of NOWAKORN

of Kenex Ltd. in Ontario, Canada, has very successfully marketed the Anka varietal of hempnut for the Canadian and American markets. Sean Crew of Hemp Oil Can in Manitoba, Canada, has also been dehulling seeds since 1999. For information on how to obtain machinery to dehull seeds on a commercial basis, contact The Galaxy Global Eatery in New York City.

Hempnuts or shelled hempseed contain as much as 25–30 percent protein. Roughly 65 percent of this total protein occurs as the easily digestible storage protein edestin. By shelling the seed it is now possible to remove most of the THC that exists on the shell. The hempnuts contain virtually no THC (less than 3 parts per million, 3ppm). The nut can no longer germinate, allowing the seeds to be imported to the U.S. without sterilization. (Currently, only sterilized seeds are allowed into the United States.)

We find these nuts the most versatile by-product of the hempseed for the restaurant's applications. Rather than deal with the pesky hulls, which are also highly nutritious, we prefer to toast, grind, and "milk" the nut for culinary delight. They can be used raw, toasted, baked, or ground and substituted for just about any other nut used in cooking. The flavor has been been described as a cross between a walnut and sesame seed. I find it particularly "hempnutty."

Nutritional Facts on Hempnuts Per 14 gram serving	
Energy	74 cal.
Protein	4.4 g
Fat	4.8 g
Polyunsaturates	3.5 g
Linoleic Acid	2.7 g
Monounsaturates	0.6 g
Saturates	0.5 g
Cholesterol	0 mg
Carbohydrate	3.2 g
Sugars	0.4 g
Dietary Fibre	2.1 g
Percentage of Recommended Daily Intake	
Vitamin E	66 %
Iron	15 %

Source: Mother Earth Enterprises, NYC, with Supermarket Testing Laboratory

Hemp Flour

Hemp flour is the finely ground seed meal that remains when seeds are pressed for oil. It typically contains 5 to 10 percent oil, with the rest being protein and hulls. To make your own hemp flour, simply toast hempseeds in an iron skillet or wok on the stove, let cool, and grind in a coffee grinder. A Corona Stone Mill Grinder or Champion grain mill attachment for your Champion Juicer (see Glossary) works much better. There are also some very good quality Amish mills available. Once the seeds are ground, be careful to sift out any remaining hulls leftover that would make the flour "gritty." Best bet is to purchase a commercial flour. We recommend "Hempola's" flour

from Ontario, Canada. Zima Food, in Manitoba, Canada, or Ruth's Foods in Ontario also provide good quality flours. (See Resources for contact information.)

Since hemp flour lacks "gluten" and has a very pungent flavor, we use hemp flour as an additive flour to unbleached white, wheat, corn, chickpea, chestnut, or rye flours. Generally we use a ratio of 5:1, with hemp flour being the additive. Rancidity is also the evil enemy of this flour, so keep it cool and dry, preferable in the freezer or refrigerator. Shelf life should be six months to a year if kept under these conditions.

Hempola Hempseed Flour	
Nutritional Facts Serving size 1/4 cup (35 g)	

Amount Per Serving	
Calories 134	Calories from Fat 32
	% Daily Value*
Total Fat** 3.6g	6%
Saturated Fat 0.4g	2%
Cholesterol 0mg	0%
Sodium 3.6mg	0%
Total Carbohydrates 11.0g	4%
Dietary Fibre 6.4g	26%
Sugars 6.4g	
Protein 14.3g	
Vitamin A 0%	Vitamin C 0%
Iron 17mg 9%	Calcium 66mg 9%

* Percents Daily Values are based on a 2,000 calorie diet. Your daily values may be higher or lower depending on your calorie needs,
** approximately 80% of which is polyunsaturated fat (Omega 6 and Omega 3 essential fatty acids and GLA)

Source: Hempola

Now that we helped answer WHAT IS HEMP . . . ? how about further details on WHY HEMP?

The most succinct answer is that hempseed is one of the best vegetable protein and essential fatty acid sources. Thus it is a great nutritional alternative to meat. For a bigger picture, consider this:

By 1985 Americans ate only half as much grains and potatoes as in 1909. Consumption of red meat skyrocketed by almost 50 percent. Poultry consumption nearly tripled. Since livestock consume grain and other food items, and require additional equipment and health care, the cumulative energy value used to produce one calorie of beef protein is seventy-eight calories of fuel. In contrast, one calorie of soybean protein takes only two calories of fuel to produce. Raising livestock for consumption of the meat uses vastly more resources, water, and land than grain and vegetable production.

If Americans reduced their intake of meat by just 10 percent, an estimated 100 million people could be adequately nourished using the land, water, and energy released from growing livestock feed and allowing animals free range.

Want more? In 1960, 13 percent of staphylococci infections were penicillin-resistant: in 1988 it was 91 percent. Today we have Mad Cow Disease. Why are germs more immune to drugs? Researchers have been contemplating overuse as a possibility. About 55 percent of antibiotics used in the U.S. are fed routinely to livestock whether the animals seem ill or not. This is partly a prophylactic measure to offset crowded and unhealthy living conditions for these animals. United States meat and pharmaceutical industries support this practice whereas the European community bans it, suspecting a natural selection process that kills off weaker germs while allowing drug-resistant germs to dominate the gene pool. This does not bode well for humans that consume these meats. Feeding livestock hempseed is a way to support their immune systems and bolster the animals' well being without the use of antibiotics unless it is absolutely necessary. Animals fed hempseed could therefore prove to be healthier and more disease-resistant, but since the method is nutritional rather than antibiotic, bacteria would not become resistant.

So, why hemp? This is good fodder to begin digesting the answer.

Conclusion

At The Galaxy Global Eatery, I believe that we have found that ONE ingredient that is innovative and progressive: A seed that has been used for thousands of years and still goes unused in America and other parts or the world when it could be a staple food. I hope this book encourages the reader to add the hempseeds, hempnuts, hempseed oil, and hemp flour to his or her pantry for many a nutritious meal to come. Remember, "You can't eat money."

Stay hempy, healthy, and wise . . .

Let the journey begin into the world of galaxy food, fun, and fine hemp cuisine.

Substitutions for the Hempseed

As I have mentioned earlier, there may be an issue with obtaining hemp food products in the United States after publication of this book. I'm very confident that the regulatory agencies of the U.S. government will have sound judgment regarding the hempseed. In the event I'm proven wrong, here is a list of substitute ingredients that one may want to use until this issue sorts itself out. Those of you in Canada, Australia, England, and Eastern Europe can disregard them unless, of course, you want to apply culinary options.

Mild Seed Substitutes:
flax seed, pine nuts, sesame seed, sunflower seed

Pungent Seed Substitutes:
caraway seed, celery seed, fennel seed, mustard seed

Nut Substitutes (Coarsely Ground):
almond, Brazil nut, cashew, hazelnut, macadamia, peanut, pecan, pistachio, pumpkin seed, walnut

Oil Substitutes:
grape seed oil, olive oil, pine nut oil, pumpkin seed oil, rape seed oil, sesame oil, walnut oil

Flour Substitutes:
black, red, or white rice flour, chick pea flour, rye flour, seven-grain flour, whole wheat flour

Keep in mind that different ingredients will most definitely effect the outcome of your culinary experimentation. All in all, the recipes are sound and should accommodate these substitutions. As hempseed purists, we of course hope that you keep to the vision we share in this cookbook, and try out this innovative ingredient.

List of Recipes

Hemp Staples

Genesis

Soothing & Refresco

Bowls, Greens, & More

Dressers

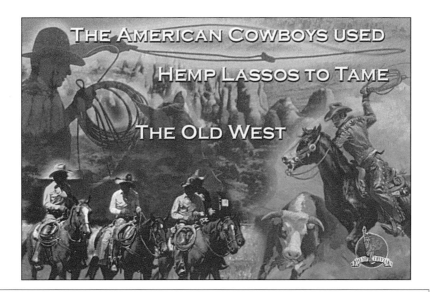

The U.S. census of 1850 counted 8,327 hemp plantations (minimum 2,000-acre farms) growing hemp for cordage, fabric, and canvas.

Stellar Starters

Quasars

Noodulars

The great writings of Lao Tsu and Confucius were transcribed on hemp paper, which doesn't turn yellow or become brittle. (*Industrial Hemp, Hemptech*)

Fish, Meat, & Poultry

Bakery

For over 200 years, you could pay your taxes with cannabis hemp anywhere in America.

The Galaxy Global Eatery

Hemp Cookbook

Hemp has lower net nutrient requirements than other common farm crops because it can return 60–70% of the nutrients it takes from the soil when dried in the field.

Hemp Staples

"*I*n the beginning, there was Hemp Milk." Here are some essential recipes that will serve as fundamental staples to be used as stocks and bases in other recipes throughout the cookbook. Included are hemp-based, dairy-free alternatives to milk, butter, cheese, and whipped cream. Keep in mind that this cookbook is "transitional" in scope and includes the use of dairy products in some recipes. At The Galaxy, we like to reach the broadest possible cross-section of diners, and so we do offer some dairy options. (Personally, I would encourage everyone to choose a low-dairy diet.) In the case of Hemp Ice Cream, you may certainly omit the cream and make a pure version of hemp ice or sorbet. Have fun, experiment with these staples, and feel free to flavor them with your favorite sweeteners or spices.

Hemp Milk

YIELDS 4 CUPS

        3 cups water
        1 cup hempnuts
        1 tablespoon agave nectar (see Glossary)

Put all the ingredients in a blender and blend until smooth.

Pour the milk through a sieve and chill.

Serve cold or use for *Galaxy Global Eatery Hemp Cookbook* recipes.

Sweet Hempnut Butter

YIELDS 1 CUP

        1 cup hempnuts
        2 teaspoons agave nectar (see Glossary) or honey
        1 teaspoon salt
        1/4 cup hempseed oil
        1/4 cup water

Toast the hempnuts in a medium-hot pan until the nut aroma can be detected.

Place the hempnuts, agave nectar, and salt in blender.

Turn blender on and slowly add hempseed oil. With the blender turned off, use a rubber spatula to help emulsify the oil and the ground hempnuts.

Add water as necessary to achieve the proper consistency, which should be slightly thicker than natural peanut butter.

Hemp Cheese

YIELDS 1 CUP

> 3 cups warm water
> 1 cup hempnuts
> 2 teaspoons salt
> 1 teaspoon cumin

Place the warm water and hempnuts in a blender and puree for 3 minutes. Drain through a fine sieve. Reserve the milk and discard the solids.

Place the milk, salt, and cumin in a sauce pan and bring to simmer. As the milk simmers it will begin to curd. Allow the process to continue until most liquid has evaporated. Strain through fine sieve again. Push the curd through the sieve.

Once the curd is completely dry, place it in a plastic-wrap lined container. Place a heavy weight, such as a book, on top to press the curd. Refrigerate for at least 24 hours.

Hemp has few weed or insect enemies, and can be grown without chemical pesticides, herbicides, fungicides, or fertilizers. By comparison, 50 percent of all pesticides are used on cotton.

Hempnut Whipped Cream

YIELDS 2 CUPS

> 1¹/2 cups hempnuts
> water to soak the hempnuts
> ¹/2 cup fresh-squeezed orange juice

Immerse the hempnuts in a bowl of water and allow them to soak for at least 2 hours. Drain the hempnuts and place them with the orange juice in a blender. Blend until white and fluffy. If the cream becomes too dry add a little more orange juice.

Hemp Ice Cream

YIELDS 1 QUART

> 2 cups Hemp Milk (page 4)
> 2 cups heavy cream
> ¹/2 vanilla bean, split from top to bottom
> 1 tablespoon hempseed oil
> 4 egg yolks
> ¹/2 cup sugar

In a small pot, heat the Hemp Milk, cream, and vanilla bean. Do not allow to boil.

Take out the vanilla bean and remove the seeds. Finely dice the vanilla bean and place it back in the milk. Add the hempseed oil. Set aside.

Mix the egg yolks and sugar in a stainless steel bowl and heat over a pot of boiling water. Add to the milk-cream mixture.

Cook the mixture on low heat stirring constantly, until it coats the back of a spoon. Strain and cool immediately.

Use an ice cream maker to freeze into ice cream. Serve when frozen.

Vegetable Stock

YIELDS 2 QUARTS

1 large carrot
2 celery stalks
2 large ripe tomatoes
1 large white onion
$1/2$ celery root
1 small turnip
1 parsnip
1 leek
1-inch piece fresh ginger
4 whole garlic cloves
1 bunch parsley
2 tablespoons juniper berries
2 bay leaves
2 tablespoons salt
10 peppercorns
1 gallon filtered water

Add all the vegetables and the water to a 2-gallon stockpot.

Add the juniper berries, bay leaves, salt, and peppercorns and boil for 10 minutes.

Reduce the heat and continue cooking for 50 minutes, or until all the vegetables are soft and the broth has good flavor. Add salt and pepper to taste.

Pour the stock through a strainer. Discard the vegetables and allow the broth to cool to room temperature. Use for *Galaxy Global Eatery Hemp Cookbook* recipes.

Refrigerate for up to 5 days.

Genesis

Nothing at The Galaxy is quite at it appears, neither in design nor wording. These items were chosen as the all-time favorite start-of-the-day recipes by our clientele — photographers, businessmen, advertising executives, filmmakers — and of course, our regulars. An ounce of hempseed oil in your choice of fresh-squeezed juice can rejuvenate body and soul for a kick-start in the morning. One of first recipes I tested was Hemp Waffles, which I introduced to my niece and nephew from New Hampshire. I still get requests from them seven years later for those "tasty waffles." Of course, no breakfast is as sound as fresh Fruit Hemp Salad drizzled with hempseed oil, accompanied by a Hempnut Muffin. Clean, simple, and energetic!

And the Earth brought forth grass and herb yielding seed after its kind and the tree yielding fruit whose seed was in itself after its kind; and God saw that it was good.—Genesis: Chapter 1, verse 12 (King James Version)

Dried Fruit Hemp Granola

YIELDS 6 CUPS

Granola

    4 tablespoons orange zest

1¹/3 cups coconut, shredded

    2 teaspoons cinnamon

    1 cup hempnuts, toasted

    1 cup pecans, chopped

    1 cup dates, pitted and chopped

    2 cups rolled oats

1¹/2 cups (3 sticks) unsalted butter, melted

   ¹/2 cup pure maple syrup

    1 cup light brown sugar, packed

Preheat oven to 300°F. Grate orange peel to yield 4 tablespoons of zest. Be careful not to grate the white pith. The pith will lend a very bitter taste to the granola.

Combine zest, coconut, cinnamon, hempnuts, pecans, dates, and rolled oats. Over low heat, combine butter, maple syrup, and light brown sugar.

Mix sugar-butter mixture with dry ingredients. Make sure the dry ingredients are fully coated with sugar-butter mixture. Spread the mixture evenly over a cookie sheet. Place in oven for 30 minutes until granola is aromatic and dry. Serve with fruit, yogurt, milk, or any fruit juices of your choice.

 Pure maple syrup is known for balancing blood sugar levels for people with hypoglycemia. It is also one of New York state's premier farm food products.

Corn Pancakes
with Apple-Cranberry Chutney

MAKES EIGHT 6-INCH PANCAKES

Pancake Batter

$^1/_2$ cup cornmeal

1 tablespoon sugar

$^1/_2$ cup unbleached white flour

2 tablespoons hemp flour

2 teaspoons baking powder

2 eggs

1 cup milk, plus more if needed

$^3/_4$ cup corn kernels, pureed

12 tablespoons ($1^1/_2$ sticks) unsalted butter, melted

extra butter for cooking

Combine the cornmeal, sugar, white and hemp flours, and baking powder.

Add the eggs, milk, and corn puree to mix. Mix in the melted butter.

Heat 1 teaspoon butter in a non-stick sauté pan. Add $^1/_4$ cup batter and cook until golden on each side. Repeat until all batter is used.

Apple-Cranberry Chutney

2 tablespoons fresh ginger, grated

1 small red onion, diced

1 tablespoon peanut oil

4–5 medium apples, peeled, cored, and diced

$^1/_2$ cup cranberries

2 limes, zest and juice

2 cups water

$^1/_2$ cup golden raisins

$^3/_4$ cup apple cider vinegar

$^3/_4$ cup raw cane sugar (see Glossary)

Sweat the ginger and red onion in peanut oil. Add the apples, cranberries, lime zest, and water. Cook until liquid evaporates and apples are soft.

Add the lime juice, golden raisins, vinegar, and sugar. Cook an additional 5 minutes, stirring frequently. Set aside.

Serve pancakes topped with chutney.

> • Cranberries are known to be a great way to flush the kidneys and help with urinary tract infections.

Hempnut Pumpkin Preserve

YIELDS 2 CUPS

> 1 pumpkin, sliced, peeled, and seeded to make 1 cup chopped pumpkin flesh
> 1 cup granulated sugar
> 2 tablespoons fresh ginger, grated
> juice of $1/2$ lemon
> $1/8$ cup hempnuts

Steam the pumpkin flesh until tender (about 15–20 minutes).

Mix the pumpkin, sugar, ginger, lemon juice, and hempnuts together in a large bowl. Wrap and leave in a cool place for 24 hours.

Transfer the pumpkin mixture to a large heavy saucepan and cook on low heat until the sugar dissolves.

Raise the heat to high and boil for 15 minutes until thick and translucent, mixing if needed.

Ladle through a funnel into a clean dry jar. Seal tightly with a wax disk, wax side down. Cover with an airtight lid.

Store in a cool dry place for at least 1 month before eating.

Ginger Buttermilk Hemp Pancakes

MAKES 8 PANCAKES

1³/4 cups cake flour
3 teaspoons baking powder
¹/2 teaspoon kosher salt
4 eggs, separated
1¹/2 cups buttermilk
¹/2 cup Hemp Milk (page 4)
¹/2 teaspoon cream of tartar
4 tablespoons (¹/2 stick) unsalted butter, melted
1 cup crystallized ginger, chopped
¹/2 cup hempnuts, toasted
extra butter for cooking

Combine cake flour, baking powder, and kosher salt in a metal bowl.

Separate the egg yolks from their whites. Combine the yolks with buttermilk and Hemp Milk. Keep separately.

Whisk egg whites by hand or in a mixer. Once the whites double in size, add the cream of tartar and whisk until whites form stiff peaks.

Slowly add the yolk-buttermilk mixture to the dry ingredients. Add melted butter and mix until the butter has been incorporated. Fold in the whites. This will make a fluffy pancake. Make sure not to overwork batter.

Fold in the ginger and toasted hempnuts.

Heat a small amount of butter in a frying pan and ladle pancake batter to desired size. Flip the pancake over when bubbles begin to form all over the top. Pancakes should be golden and fluffy.

> Ginger is a warming herb used to treat PMS, morning sickness, and general nausea. It is also improves circulation and cleanses the colon. It is a natural diuretic.

Hemp Waffles

MAKES 9 WAFFLES

2¹/₂ cups unbleached white flour
¹/₂ cup cups hemp flour
1¹/₄ cups cornstarch
¹/₄ cup sugar
1 teaspoon salt
4 cups warm water
6 eggs
12 tablespoons (1¹/₂ sticks) unsalted butter, melted
2 teaspoons vanilla extract
non-stick cooking spray

Sift together the white and hemp flours with the cornstarch.

Stir in the sugar and salt.

Make a well in the center of the flour mixture and slowly whisk in the water.

Whisk in the eggs, butter, and vanilla. Stir until you have a smooth batter (about 3 minutes).

Cover and let mixture rest 30 minutes before using. If the batter is too thin, sprinkle with a little more flour and whisk in until smooth.

Heat oven to 250°F for storing finished waffles until serving.

Heat a waffle maker and spray with non-stick spray.

Make waffles until the batter is used up, keeping them warm in the oven. Serve with maple syrup, fruits, jams, ice cream, or whipped cream.

> ● Hemp foods go far beyond the breakfast of champions for nutrition without containing GMOs (Genetically Modified Organisms) for healthy bodies and souls.

Nutmeg French Toast
with Maple-Hemp Butter

MAKES 8 PIECES OF FRENCH TOAST

Nutmeg French Toast

8 thick slices of bread (such as challah)

6 eggs

1 cup heavy cream

2 cups Hemp Milk (page 4)

1/2 teaspoon vanilla extract

1/3 cup sugar

1 tablespoon cinnamon

1 teaspoon nutmeg

1 tablespoon unsalted butter

Mix together the eggs, cream, milk, vanilla, sugar, cinnamon, and nutmeg.

Soak the bread in egg mixture. Coat both sides evenly. Place a frying pan over medium heat and add butter. Place the Nutmeg French Toast in the pan and brown on both sides. Make sure egg mixture is cooked through.

Maple-Hemp Butter

8 tablespoons (1 stick) unsalted butter, softened

1/4 cup pure maple syrup

1/8 cup hempseed oil

2 tablespoons hempnuts, toasted

Place softened butter in bowl. Add maple syrup, hempseed oil, and toasted hempnuts. Use an electric mixer or wooden spoon to incorporate the ingredients evenly. Place the mixture on parchment paper or wax paper and roll up like a sausage. Refrigerate until butter is firm.

To serve, slice slabs from the Maple-Hemp Butter log. Place on top of hot Nutmeg French Toast and allow to melt. Serve with syrup or fruit.

Hempnut Chickpea Crêpes

with Pear-Date Relish & Hoisin Tofu Crème Anglaise

SERVES 6

Hempnut Chickpea Crêpes

> 1 cup chickpea flour
> 1 cup unbleached white flour
> 1 teaspoon salt
> 2 tablespoons extra-virgin olive oil
> 2 cups warm water
> 2 tablespoons hempnuts

Whisk the chickpea flour, white flour, and salt together in a bowl. Add the oil and water and whisk to combine. Transfer to a blender and blend in the hempnuts until all the ingredients are mixed together well. Allow the batter to rest for at least 20 minutes.

Heat a non-stick pan and oil lightly. Pour $1/4$ cup of the batter into the pan in a circular motion so that the batter covers the entire surface. Flip the crêpe when it starts to bubble and becomes golden around the edges. Cook the other side for about 30 seconds. Transfer to a plate and repeat with remaining batter.

Pear-Date Relish

> 2 tablespoons unsalted butter
> $1/4$ teaspoon crushed dried red chilies
> 1 tablespoon fresh ginger, minced
> $1/2$ tablespoon orange zest
> $1/4$ teaspoon crushed cardamom seeds
> 2-inch piece cinnamon stick
> $1/2$ cup fresh-squeezed orange juice
> $1/4$ cup light brown sugar, packed
> 6–7 medium bosc pears, peeled, quartered, cored, and cut crosswise into $1/3$-inch slices
> $1/2$ cup soft dates, pitted and cut into small pieces
> $1/3$ cup hempnuts, toasted

Melt the butter in a saucepan and add the red chilies, ginger, orange zest, cardamom seeds, and cinnamon. Fry for 1 or 2 minutes to release the flavors.

Add the orange juice and sugar, stirring until the sugar dissolves. Stir in the pears, bring to a gentle boil, and cook until syrupy and thick.

Remove the pan from the heat, then stir in the dates and hempnuts.

Set aside and allow to cool to room temperature.

Hoisin Tofu Crème Anglaise

    8 ounce package soft silken tofu
    $1/4$ cup hoisin sauce (see Glossary)
    $1/4$ cup water
    1 tablespoon vanilla extract
    2 tablespoons granulated sugar

Blend all ingredients together in a blender until smooth. Adjust the sugar and vanilla extract to taste. Set aside to cool.

Serve the crêpes, using the Pear-Date Relish as a filling. Top with Hoisin Tofu Crème Anglaise.

Betsy Ross crafted the first American flag out of hemp.

Fruit Hemp Salad

SERVES 8

2 cups blueberries
2 cups raspberries
1 cup blackberries
1/2 cup watermelon balls
1 medium mango
1 small cantaloupe
2 cups strawberries, quartered
1 cup grape tomatoes, seeded
1 avocado, peeled and diced
3/8 cup mirin (see Glossary)
3/8 cup fresh-squeezed orange juice
1-inch piece ginger, grated
15 mint leaves, thinly sliced
1/8 cup hempseed oil

Place the blueberries, raspberries, and blackberries in a bowl.

Remove the watermelon from its rind with a melon baller. Peel the mango and separate the flesh from the pit, then dice. Cut the cantaloupe in half. Remove the seeds and cut flesh from rind with a melon baller. Slice the strawberries. Add all the fruit together in one bowl.

Cut the grape tomatoes in half. Add tomatoes and avocado to the fruit mix.

Add the mirin, orange juice, grated ginger, and mint leaves.

Add the hempseed oil and gently mix all ingredients. Allow mixture to sit at room temperature or refrigerate for at least 1 hour before serving.

Roasted Artichoke Hemp Frittata

MAKES ONE 6-INCH FRITTATA

>   1 medium artichoke
>   1 tablespoon vegetable oil
> $^1/_2$ roasted red pepper
>   2 asparagus stalks
>   3 eggs
> $^1/_4$ cup Hemp Milk (page 4)
>   1 tablespoon hempseed oil
> $^1/_4$ cup hempnuts, toasted
>   2 tablespoons Hemp Cheese (page 5)

Carefully clean and peel one artichoke, removing the choke. Cut the artichoke into six pieces, lengthwise. Heat a frying pan over medium-high heat and add vegetable oil, then the sliced artichoke. Reduce heat to medium-low. Cook until brown and tender (about 8 minutes). Set aside.

Oil and salt a red pepper and place it over an open flame, turning until the skin begins to blister on all four sides. Place in a bowl and cover with plastic wrap. After 15 minutes, peel and discard the seeds. Dice into $^1/_2$-inch squares.

Place 2 stalks of asparagus in salted boiling water. Cook for $1^1/_2$ minutes, then transfer to an ice bath. Dice stalks into $^1/_4$-inch sticks.

Crack the eggs into a bowl and whisk. Add the Hemp Milk, hempseed oil, and toasted hempnuts.

Place a non-stick pan over medium heat. Add the artichokes, asparagus, and red pepper. Add whisked eggs and stir with a heat resistant rubber spatula until the eggs set. Turn off the flame and cover the pan with a lid. Wait about 3 minutes for the eggs to finish cooking.

To serve, slice the frittata and sprinkle Hemp Cheese on top.

> Red peppers are high in vitamin C and bioflavinoids (vitamin P), which are good for production of collagen and healthy skin.

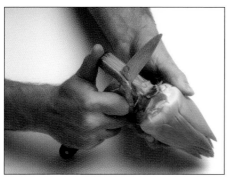

Soothing & Refresco

Refresco is a term for simple fruit cocktails in Latin America. They are big favorites at The Galaxy's bar. Agave nectar and fruit blended together have become the modest DNA for many concoctions heralded by our clientele. (As of this writing, however, there is a serious shortage of agave nectar due to drought and pestilence—and its future is in doubt.) In this section we focus on the most-asked-for drinks (warm and cold) in our extensive inventory of non-alcoholic hemp beverages. After a cold walk in the snowy Northeast, my personal favorite is the Indian Hemp Chai. Soothing for sure. For those of you sitting on the beach in Hawaii, try one of our Hemp Fruit Smoothies and get refreshed before catching The Big One. Refresco!

Hemp Chai Tea Base

MAKES TWO 6-OUNCE SERVINGS

1³/4 cups water
¹/2 cup hempnuts

Combine water and hempnuts in a small saucepan. Bring to a boil over high heat. Reduce heat to low, cover, and simmer for 5 minutes.

Strain mixture through a fine sieve, discarding remaining hempnuts. Let stand 5 minutes, then skim off thin fat layer. This base is best used the same day it is made.

Note: Try adding these, or your own favorite ingredients, to steep in this Hemp Chai Tea Base:
Fresh berries (ie. raspberries, blackberries, strawberries)
Other mixtures (ie. chopped apples & cinnamon, oranges & cloves)
Tropical fruit combinations (ie. pineapple or mango with coconut milk)
Fresh mint leaves with lemon and honey

Indian Hemp Chai

MAKES TWO 6-OUNCE SERVINGS

1 recipe Hemp Chai Tea Base (page 26)
2 whole cloves
4 whole black peppers
4 cardamom pods
1 cinnamon stick, broken into pieces
1/4 teaspoon fennel seeds
1-inch piece fresh ginger, peeled
1/8 teaspoon allspice
1/4 cup soy milk
2 tablespoons honey

Combine Hemp Chai Tea Base, cloves, black peppers, cardamom pods, cinnamon stick, fennel seeds, ginger, and allspice.

Bring to a boil over high heat. Turn off heat and let steep for 5 minutes.

Strain through a fine sieve. Stir in milk and honey. Serve hot.

Golden Ginger Hemp Tea

MAKES TWO 6-OUNCE SERVINGS

1 recipe Hemp Chai Tea Base (page 26)
2–3 tablespoons fresh ginger, finely chopped
2 tablespoons fresh-squeezed lemon juice
2 tablespoons honey

Bring Hemp Chai Tea Base to a boil in a small saucepan. Remove from heat and stir in ginger, lemon juice, and honey. Let steep for 5 minutes. Strain and serve hot.

Black Tapioca & Hemp Milk Jasmine Tea

MAKES TWO 6-OUNCE SERVINGS

>   1/2 cup black tapioca pearls
>   1/2 cup sugar
>   3 cups water
>   4 cups jasmine tea
>   2 cups Hemp Milk (page 4)
>   2 tablespoons agave nectar (see Glossary) or honey, or to taste

Boil tapioca pearls according to the directions on the bag. (Each manufacturer of pearls is different and therefore it is best to follow the particular maker's instructions.) Set aside.

Make a simple syrup by combining the sugar and water in a saucepan. Boil for 10 minutes. Set aside to cool. Allow tapioca pearls to absorb the sweetness of the simple syrup.

Steep jasmine tea and reduce by two-thirds. Add it to the Hemp Milk and puree in a blender. Add agave nectar or honey to taste. Shake in a martini shaker with ice and pour in a glass. Spoon in tapioca pearls. Serve cold.

Hemp Coffee

SERVES 4

3/4 cup premium coffee beans, ground
1/4 cup milled hempseed, toasted
4 cups purified water
raw cane sugar (see Glossary) to taste
Hemp Milk (page 4) or soy milk to taste

Pour the water into a coffee or espresso machine to be heated.
    Mix the coffee and milled hempseed together until well combined.
    Brew the coffee as per machine's instructions.
    Sweeten by adding sugar and Hemp Milk or soy milk to taste. Serve.

Hemp Hot Chocolate

SERVES 4

2 cups Hemp Milk (page 4)
2 cups soy milk
1/2 cup chocolate sauce

Mix the hemp and soy milks together and heat to just under boiling point.
    Mix in the chocolate sauce and serve.

Hemp Power Smoothie

MAKES TWO 16-OUNCE SMOOTHIES

1 small banana
4 small strawberries
$1/2$ small mango
$1/3$ cup plain yogurt
$1/8$ cup hempnuts
$1/3$ cup crushed ice
1 tablespoon agave nectar (see Glossary)

Add the banana, strawberries, mango, and yogurt together in a blender and blend until smooth.

Add the hempnuts, crushed ice, and agave nectar. Blend until smooth. Serve.

Mango Smoothie

MAKES TWO 16-OUNCE SMOOTHIES

2 small mangos, peeled and pitted
$1/4$ cup hempnuts
1 cup plain yogurt
1 cup ice cubes
2 tablespoons agave nectar (see Glossary)

Blend all ingredients in a blender until smooth.

Adjust sweetness to taste and serve with a few slices of mango on top.

Blueberry Smoothie

MAKES TWO 16-OUNCE SMOOTHIES

> 1 cup blueberries
> 1/4 cup hempnuts
> 1 cup plain yogurt
> 1 cup ice cubes
> 2 tablespoons agave nectar (see Glossary)

Blend all ingredients in a blender until smooth.
Adjust sweetness to taste and serve with a few blueberries on top.

Strawberry Smoothie

MAKES TWO 16-OUNCE SMOOTHIES

> 2 cups strawberries
> 1 small banana
> 1/4 cup hempnuts
> 1 cup plain yogurt
> 1 cup ice cubes
> 2 tablespoons agave nectar (see Glossary)

Blend all ingredients in a blender until smooth.
Adjust sweetness to taste and serve with a few sliced strawberries on top.

Rejuvenation Tonic

MAKES TWO 16-OUNCE TONICS

$1/2$ beet, peeled and cut into small pieces
1 medium Granny Smith apple, peeled, cored, and chopped
2 cups fresh-squeezed orange juice
1 cup ice cubes
$1/4$ cup hempnuts
1 teaspoon fresh ginger, minced
1 tablespoon hempseed oil

Place the beet, apple, orange juice, and ice in a blender. Puree until smooth.

With blender on medium, add the hempnuts and fresh ginger, then slowly add the hempseed oil until blended. Serve.

Gingered Melon Hempade

MAKES TWO 16-OUNCE HEMPADES

$3/4$ cup honeydew melon, chopped
1 large cucumber
1 teaspoon fresh ginger, minced
$1/2$ pinch ground cinnamon
1 cup ice cubes
1 tablespoon hempseed oil

Separate the pulp of the melon and cucumber from the juice in a Champion Juicer (see Glossary). Transfer the juices to a blender and blend with the fresh ginger, cinnamon, and ice in a blender.

With the blender on a low speed, slowly add the hempseed oil until emulsified. Serve.

Lemon-Blueberry Hempade

MAKES TWO 16-OUNCE HEMPADES

juice of 1 lemon
zest of $^1/_2$ lemon
2 tablespoons raw cane sugar (see Glossary)
1 teaspoon hempseed oil
$^1/_2$ cup water
7 blueberries
2 mint leaves, thinly sliced
1 cup ice cubes

Add the lemon juice, lemon zest, and sugar in a blender and blend until smooth. Slowly add the hempseed oil with the blender on a low speed until emulsified, then add the water.

Turn the blender off and add the blueberries and mint leaves. Pulse on and off 5 times until just mixed.

Pour the juice through a sieve over the ice cubes. Serve.

THE CHINESE HAVE USED HEMP FOR CENTURIES

The Chinese character "Ma" was the earliest name for hemp.

Bowls, Greens, & More

Here we've chosen our most popular soups and salads, with emphasis on the global character of past and present Galaxy menus. We've explored pumpkin seed oil from Austria, traditional French influences with our goat cheese salads, American recipes made with Northwestern wild rices, Mexican yellow tomato gazpacho, California avocado, jicama, and chayote, South American quinoa, Italian arugula, Asian lychee nuts, and Chinese long beans. We would have liked to have spent months traveling through the culinary world—from Thailand to Iceland. Time hasn't allowed such extensive exploration, but we've managed to savor the most interesting of the world of soups and salads and blend them with hempseed for your midday delight. I find the most interesting recipe in this section to be the Mango-Rosewater Soup—heaven on earth with subtle culinary nuance.

Mellow Yellow Gazpacho

Serves 6

> 1 medium cantaloupe, peeled and seeded
> 1 medium yellow pepper, seeded
> 4 medium yellow tomatoes
> 1 medium seedless cucumber, peeled
> 1 small white sweet onion, chopped
> 1 garlic clove, minced
> 1/3 cup hempseed oil
> salt and pepper to taste
> 1 small bunch chives, thinly sliced, for garnish

Add all ingredients except the hempseed oil to a food processor and blend until smooth.

Pass the mixture through a sieve, then return to the food processor.

Blend on medium and slowly add the hempseed oil. Add salt and pepper to taste.

Refrigerate until cold and garnish with chives.

Cantaloupes are very high in vitamin A. They are very cooling to the body and excellent for lowering fevers.

Gingered Carrot & Beet Soup

SERVES 6

>1 cup ginger, peeled and sliced
>5 cups water
>2 pounds carrots, peeled
>1 pound beets
> salt and pepper to taste
>2 tablespoons cilantro leaves, coarsely chopped for garnish
>2 tablespoons hempseed oil

Place ginger slices in a small saucepan with 5 cups of water. Bring to a simmer and cook over medium heat until the water reduces by half. Strain and discard the ginger. Set the ginger water aside.

Preheat oven to 400°F.

Cut the carrots into 1-inch pieces and wrap in foil. Wrap the beets in foil. Place on a baking sheet and bake for 1 hour, or until the vegetables are tender. Allow to cool.

Peel the beets. Puree the carrots and beets in a food processor until smooth. While processing, add 1 cup of the ginger water.

Combine the carrot-beet puree with the rest of the ginger water in a large bowl. Add salt and pepper to taste.

Serve hot or cold. To serve cold, chill at least 4 hours. Serve sprinkled with cilantro leaves and drizzled with hempseed oil.

Red beets are high in vitamin A and iron. They are excellent for cleansing the liver, heart, and blood.

Roasted Butternut Squash Soup

Serves 6

> 2 tablespoons butter
> 2 leeks, diced
> 1 celery stalk, diced
> 2 carrots, peeled and diced
> 4 whole garlic cloves
> 8 cups butternut squash, cut into cubes
> 1 bay leaf
> 2 pieces star anise
> 1/2 cinnamon stick
> 2 teaspoons allspice
> 8 cups water
> 1 baking potato, diced
> 1 cup cream or soy milk
> 1 recipe Manchego Hemp Tuile (page 236)

Preheat the oven to 375°F. Melt the butter in a 3-quart pot over medium heat. Add the leeks, celery, carrots, and whole garlic cloves. Cook for about 5 minutes. The vegetables should start to emit an aromatic fragrance.

Add squash, bay leaf, star anise, cinnamon stick, and allspice. Cook for an additional 5 minutes.

Add water and bring to a simmer for 25–30 minutes. Add the diced potato and cook an additional 10 minutes.

Carefully place the mixture, one batch at a time, in a blender and puree for 2 minutes per batch. Strain through a sieve. Whisk in cream or soy milk.

To serve, ladle the soup into a serving bowl. Float Manchego Hemp Tuile in center of bowl and sprinkle chives over soup.

> Butternut squash is high in vitamin A. Chinese pharmacopoeia suggests that it is good for the spleen and stomach.

Corn Chowder
with Tomato Raft

SERVES 6

Corn Chowder

> 1 tablespoon vegetable oil
> 1 tablespoon garlic, minced
> 1 large Spanish onion, chopped
> 2 bay leaves
> 15 ears corn, kernels removed
> 2 medium potatoes, peeled and diced small
> 1 bunch scallions, sliced thinly
> 8 cups water
> 1 teaspoon ground cumin
> 1 tablespoon fresh parsley, chopped
> 1 tablespoon dried thyme
> 3 tablespoons hempseed oil
> 1/2 cup hempnuts
> salt and pepper to taste
> 1/2 bunch scallions, thinly sliced, for garnish

Heat the vegetable oil in a large sauce pan. Sauté the garlic, onion, and bay leaves until onion is translucent.

Add the scallions, corn, potatoes, and water to the pan.

Bring to a boil and cook for 20 minutes, or until the potatoes are tender.

Remove half of the mixture to a food processor and process to a coarse puree.

Return the puree to the soup.

Add the parsley, cumin, thyme, hempnuts, and salt and pepper to taste.

Reduce to a simmer and cook for 15 minutes. Add the hempseed oil.

Tomato Raft

       3 plum tomatoes

       3 tablespoons olive oil

       2 garlic cloves, minced

         salt and pepper to taste

Preheat oven to 350°F.

Slice the tomatoes in half and drizzle them with olive oil. Spread with garlic and salt and pepper to taste.

Arrange the tomatoes on a wire rack and bake in the preheated oven for 2 minutes. Remove from the oven and allow to cool.

To serve, portion the soup into 6 bowls. Top each with a tomato raft and sprinkle with scallions.

Garlic, the "stinking rose," helps in the stimulation of digestion and helps protect the body against infections, intestinal parasites, and general pathogens. Garlic also has anti-fungal agents that help rid the body of most pathogenic fungi like Athlete's Foot and Candida. It also helps in lowering blood pressure and blood serum cholesterol levels.

Roasted Pumpkin Soup

SERVES 8

> 7–8 pounds pumpkin, cut into 2-inch cubes
> 1 tablespoon peanut oil
> 1 tablespoon garlic, chopped
> 1 large Spanish onion, diced
> 2 pieces star anise
> 4 cups water
> 4 cups heavy cream or soy milk
>   salt and pepper to taste
> 1 teaspoon pumpkin oil, for garnish
> 1 recipe Fried Hempnut Crisps (page 225)

Lightly oil, salt, and pepper the pumpkin cubes on a baking sheet. Place in a 350°F oven and cook approximately 35–40 minutes, or until tender. Remove and mash by hand in a bowl.

Add peanut oil, garlic, and onion to a medium stockpot. Sauté approximately 5–6 minutes, until onion is translucent. Add the water, heavy cream, star anise, and pumpkin.

Allow ingredients to come to a boil and reduce to a simmer for 30 minutes. Stir frequently so pumpkin does not burn on bottom.

Remove from heat, then puree in blender or food processor. Use care when blending hot ingredients: vent the top and use a low speed.

To serve, ladle the soup out into bowls and drizzle the surface with pumpkin oil. Top with Fried Hempnut Crisps.

Tomato Basil Soup

SERVES 6

    2 tablespoons butter
    1 small white onion, minced
    2 garlic cloves, minced
    6 vine ripe tomatoes, chopped
    1 tablespoon tomato paste
    1 bunch fresh basil, chopped
    1 recipe Vegetable Stock (page 7)
    3 tablespoons raw cane sugar
    1 teaspoon ground cumin
    1 teaspoon ground nutmeg
    1/2 cup hempnuts
    salt and pepper to taste
    6 teaspoons hempseed oil
    3 garlic cloves, very thinly sliced

Heat the butter in a pot and sauté the onion and minced garlic until translucent.

Add the chopped tomatoes and tomato paste and cook for 5 minutes.

Add half the basil and cook for an additional 5 minutes.

Add the vegetable stock, sugar, cumin, nutmeg, and hempnuts. Cook for 20 minutes. Add salt and pepper to taste.

Reduce the heat to medium-low.

Heat the hempseed oil in a sauté pan and fry the garlic until golden. Transfer the garlic to paper towels and set aside for garnish, reserving the oil.

Add the rest of the basil to the soup and cook until the soup has a thick consistency and is rich in flavor.

To serve, ladle soup into individual serving bowls. Garnish with a few garlic chips and 1/2 teaspoon of the garlic-hempseed oil.

Mango-Rose Water Soup

SERVES 4

Rose Water

> 1 fragrant rose
> 1 cup boiled water

Make the rose water by removing the petals from the rose. Add the rose petals to the boiled water. Cover with plastic wrap and allow to cool. Strain the water and set aside.

Mango-Rose Water Soup

> 4 medium mangos
> 4 fresh apricots, pitted
> 1-inch piece fresh ginger
> 2 teaspoons rose water
> 10 mint leaves
> 3 cups Hemp Milk (page 4)
> 4 rambutan or lychee (see Glossary)
> 4 strawberries

Peel and remove the flesh from the mangos. Remove the pits from the apricots and puree both fruits in a blender until smooth.

Add fresh ginger, rose water, mint leaves, and hemp milk, then puree until smooth.

To serve, ladle the chilled soup into a soup bowl. Place peeled rambutan or lychee in the center and garnish with sliced strawberries.

Chilled Hemp Apple Soup
with Dried Apple Rings

SERVES 6

Dried Apple Rings

> 1 medium Granny Smith apple, cored

Preheat the oven to 225°F. Slice the large apple vertically, the thinner the better. Place the slices on a wire rack set over a baking tray.

Place in the oven to dry for 30–60 minutes, or until the apple slices are completely dry, turning once during cooking.

Remove the apple slices from the wire rack and cool on wax paper. Set aside.

Chilled Hemp Apple Soup

> 1 tablespoon butter
> 1 medium onion, chopped
> $^1/_2$ cup hempnuts
> 1 tablespoon mild curry powder
> $2^1/_4$ pounds Granny Smith apples, peeled, cored, and chopped
> $4^1/_2$ cups Vegetable Stock (page 7)
> salt and pepper to taste
> $^3/_4$ cup Hemp Milk (page 4)
> juice of 2 lemons

Melt the butter in a saucepan and sweat the onion. Add the hempnuts and curry powder and cook for 2 minutes.

Add chopped apples, Vegetable Stock, and salt and pepper to taste.

Bring the mixture to a boil and simmer covered for about 1 hour.

Puree the soup in a blender. Strain through a sieve and set aside to cool.

Add the Hemp Milk and fresh lemon juice to taste.

Place the soup in the refrigerator to cool.

Serve in chilled bowls with the Dried Apple Rings as a garnish.

Watercress & Chayote Salad

SERVES 6 TO 8

4 bunches watercress
2 chayotes
2 oranges, segmented
1/2 cup pecans
3/8 cup fresh-squeezed orange juice
1/8 cup tamari sauce (see Glossary)
1 teaspoon fresh ginger, grated
1/4 cup hempseed oil
2 tablespoons hempnuts, toasted
salt and pepper to taste

Wash and dry watercress thoroughly. Peel and cut chayotes into thin sticks. Try to rid the orange of as much of its white pith as possible, and segment. Combine watercress, chayote, orange segments, and pecans in a bowl.

Combine the orange juice, tamari sauce, and grated ginger in a separate bowl. Slowly stir in hempseed oil. Toss with salad ingredients. Sprinkle with hempnuts and season with salt and pepper to taste.

It was once required in Europe for monks to have three daily meals made of hempseed, whether in soups, gruel, or porridges.—Kenneth Jones, *Nutritional and Medicinal Guide to Hemp Seed,* 1995

Avocado Salad

<small>SERVES 4</small>

> 3 ears corn
> 1 medium cucumber, diced
> 1 medium red onion
> 1/4 cup loosely packed mint, cut chiffonade (see Glossary)
> 1/4 cup hempnuts
> 1/4 cup hempseed oil
>   salt and pepper to taste
> 1 cup balsamic vinegar
> 4 medium avocados
>   juice of 2 limes
> 1/2 pound mesclun greens

Shuck the corn and roast on a grill for 10 minutes. Remove the corn kernels from cob by running a knife alongside the cob.

Peel and dice the cucumber and red onion into corn kernel sized cubes.

Combine the mint, corn, cucumber, hempnuts, and red onion in bowl and mix in the hempseed oil. Season with salt and pepper to taste.

Reduce 1 cup of balsamic vinegar over medium heat, until it is syrupy (about 12 minutes). Allow to cool.

Slice the avocados into halves. Carefully remove skin so that the halves maintain their shape. Drizzle a little lime juice over each half to prevent browning.

To serve, place washed mesclun greens in the center of a serving plate. Fill the avocado halves with the corn-mint salsa and arrange on top of the greens. Drizzle with balsamic glaze.

> Avocados are very nutritious and satisfying fruits. They are an excellent source of lecithin, an important nutrient for the brain and nerve cells. Higher in vitamin A, vitamin E, and potassium than many other fruits, they also contain copper, which plays a big role in building blood. They are helpful in regulating a healthy liver, lubricating the intestines, and remedying ulcers.

Jicama, Snow Pea, & Watercress Salad

SERVES 6

1 medium jicama, cut julienne
1 medium bosc pear, peeled and cut julienne
1 medium celery root, cut julienne
24 snow peas, cut julienne
1 small red bell pepper, diced
2 bunches watercress
1 medium avocado, diced and sprinkled with lemon juice
   salt and pepper to taste
1 head Boston bibb lettuce
12 cilantro sprigs
1 recipe Hempnut Watercress-Avocado Dressing (page 68)

Combine the jicama, pear, celery root, snow peas, and red bell pepper in a bowl and toss.

Reserve a few leaves of watercress and tear the rest into small pieces. Add to the bowl with the avocado and toss gently. Add salt and pepper to taste.

To serve, arrange the Boston bibb lettuce leaves on a serving plate. Mound the salad in the center. Top with the reserved watercress and cilantro leaves. Dress with Hempnut Watercress-Avocado Dressing.

Spinach, Mandarins, & Pumpkin Seed Salad
with Agave Nectar-Mustard Vinaigrette

SERVES 6

Agave Nectar-Mustard Vinaigrette

$^{1}/3$ cup organic apple cider vinegar

2 tablespoons agave nectar (see Glossary)

2 tablespoons whole grain mustard

4 fresh thyme sprigs

$^{1}/2$ cup extra virgin olive oil

salt and pepper to taste

Add the apple cider vinegar, agave nectar, mustard, and thyme to a blender and blend until smooth.

Add the oil with the blender on a low speed until emulsified. Add salt and pepper to taste. Set aside to toss with salad.

Salad Mixings

$1^{1}/2$ pounds baby spinach leaves

$^{1}/2$ cup raw pumpkin seeds

$^{1}/2$ cup mandarin orange segments

1 recipe Hemp Cheese (page 5)

Toss the vinaigrette with the spinach in a large bowl. To serve, place the spinach in the center of a plate. Arrange the pumpkin seeds and mandarins around the salad. Sprinkle Hemp Cheese over the top.

> ● Spinach is high in iron and chlorophyll, which makes it a blood builder. It is a natural source of sulfur. In Eastern medicine it is used both as a diuretic and a laxative. Its cooling nature helps rid the blood of toxins that cause skin disease and inflammation. Spinach is also helpful in quenching diabetic thirst.

Hempnut-Crusted Goat Cheese Salad
with Fig-Balsamic Vinaigrette

SERVES 6

Hempnut-Crusted Goat Cheese
        12 ounces quality goat cheese
            salt and pepper to taste
        1 cup white unbleached flour
        2 eggs, beaten
        1 cup hempnuts
        1/2 cup coconut oil or other high-temperature frying oil

Season the goat cheese with salt and pepper to taste. Roll the cheese into twelve 1-ounce balls. Place the white flour, beaten eggs, and hempnuts in 3 separate bowls. Dredge the goat cheese balls one by one, by placing them first in the flour, then the egg, and then in the hempnuts. Heat the coconut or frying oil in a sauté pan and fry the goat cheese balls until golden brown on all sides. Transfer to paper towels to absorb excess oil. Set aside.

Fig-Balsamic Vinaigrette
        1/3 cup dried figs, chopped
        1/3 cup balsamic vinegar
        1 tablespoon Dijon mustard
        2 tablespoons berry jam
        2 teaspoons dried herbs de Provence (see Glossary)
        1/4 cup hempseed oil
        1/2 cup olive oil
            salt and pepper to taste

Add the figs, balsamic vinegar, Dijon mustard, berry jam, and herbs de Provence to a blender and blend until smooth. With the blender on a low speed, add the hempseed and olive oils and blend until emulsified. Add salt and pepper to taste. Set aside to toss with salad.

Salad Mixings

        6 medium beets
        2 tablespoons olive oil
        1 pound mustard greens, washed and chopped into bite size pieces
        3 vine ripe tomatoes, cut into wedges (six per tomato)

Preheat the oven to 450°F. Toss the beets with the olive oil and roast in the oven for about 45 minutes, or until soft. Remove from oven and allow to cool.

Peel the beets and slice into $1/2$-inch discs. Toss the mustard greens with the Fig-Balsamic Vinaigrette.

To serve, arrange the mustard greens in the middle of a serving plate. Place the goat cheese balls in the center of the greens and lay the beets and tomato wedges alternating around the cheese. Top with freshly ground pepper.

Hemp Potato & Chinese Long Bean Salad

SERVES 6

        1 pound red bliss potatoes
        1 pound Chinese long beans or haricots verts (see Glossary)
        18 asparagus stalks
        $1/4$ cup golden raisins
        1 recipe Lemon-Ginger Hemp Aioli (page 79)
        2 tablespoons hempnuts

Boil the potatoes until tender. Boil the long beans and asparagus separately in salted water until tender. Remove to an ice bath.

Cut the vegetables into bite-sized pieces and place in a bowl with the golden raisins.

Mix in the Lemon-Ginger Hemp Aioli and sprinkle with hempnuts. Serve.

Arugula & Snow Pea Blossom Salad
with Pumpkin Oil Pesto

SERVES 6

Salad Mixings

> 2 bunches arugula, cleaned and trimmed
> 1 bunch snow pea blossoms

Toss arugula and snow pea blossoms together. Set aside.

Pumpkin Oil Pesto

> 1 bunch scallions
> 2 tablespoons garlic, chopped
> $^1/4$ cup hempnuts
> $^3/4$ cup pumpkin oil
> salt and pepper to taste

Rinse the scallions, then blanch them for several seconds in boiling hot water. Remove to an ice bath.

Combine scallions, garlic, and hempnuts in a blender and blend on low. Add pumpkin oil until it begins to emulsify. Add salt and pepper to taste.

To serve, add 3 tablespoons of Pumpkin Oil Pesto to the salad combination and toss. Arrange on a serving plate and garnish with hempnuts.

Sprouted Quinoa Salad
with Hemp Mojo Dressing

SERVES 6

Sprouted Quinoa

$1/2$ cup sprouted quinoa

Put quinoa in a jar filled with water and let it soak for 2 hours. Drain through a sieve and let it sit at room temperature overnight.

The next day put the quinoa in a fresh bowl of water and mix with your fingers. Drain through a sieve. Refrigerate in a sealed jar. The sprouts are ready when they are two to three times longer than the original grain.

Salad Mixings

30 grape tomatoes, cut in half
$1/2$ seedless cucumber, diced
1 chayote, peeled and diced
1 medium beet, peeled and diced
1 small bunch mint leaves, minced

Combine all the ingredients together, then add the sprouted quinoa.

Hemp Mojo Dressing

$1/4$ cup fresh-squeezed lime juice
$1/2$ cup fresh-squeezed orange juice
4 tablespoons hempseed oil
1 small garlic clove, minced
$1/2$ small red onion, minced
1 tablespoon oregano
1 teaspoon ground cumin
zest of 1 orange
salt and pepper to taste

Put the lime and orange juices in a blender and blend. With the blender on a low speed, add the hempseed oil and blend until emulsified. Transfer the mixture to a jar. Add the minced garlic, onion, oregano, cumin, and orange zest. Add salt and pepper to taste. Store in refrigerator for up to 2 days.

Serve salad once all the ingredients are combined. Dress the salad with the Hemp Mojo Dressing and arrange on a serving plate. Top with mint leaves.

> Quinoa is the ancient food of the Inca nation. It has two times the protein of barley, corn, or rice and is alkaline-forming. Quinoa contains vitamin E and B-complex vitamins, iron, phosphorous, and more calcium than milk. Quinoa is strengthening for the entire body and specifically tones the kidneys.

Beet Tartare

SERVES 2

> 1 large beet, diced
> 1/4 cup celeriac (celery root), diced
> 1/4 cup red onion, diced
> 8 mint leaves, thinly sliced
> 1 teaspoon serrano chilies (optional to taste)
> 1 recipe Grapefruit Hemp Citronette (page 70)
> 1 medium avocado

Boil the beet until tender. Dice and combine the beet, celeriac, red onion, mint, and chilies together. Toss the tartare ingredients with the Grapefruit Hemp Citronette.

Slice the avocado in half and remove pit and skin without losing the shape of the avocado. Cut the halves lengthwise in 1/8-inch slices. Fan the slices on a plate. Top with the Beet Tartare, and serve.

Wild Rice Salad
with Cumin Hemp Vinaigrette

SERVES 4

Wild Rice Salad

    1^1/$_2$ cups wild rice

    4^1/$_2$ cups water

     2 ears corn

     1 asparagus stalk, diced

     1 small fennel bulb, diced

     1 roasted red pepper, diced

Cook the wild rice in the salted water over medium-low heat for about 1 hour. Wild rice is properly cooked when the rice grains begin to burst.

Boil the corn, asparagus, and fennel bulbs separately in salted water. Cook until tender, then remove to an ice bath. Remove corn kernels from cob by running a knife alongside the cob. Dice the fennel and asparagus. Then combine the three vegetables together and set aside.

Oil, salt, and pepper the red pepper. Place on an open flame and turn so the skin to bubbles and burns on all sides. Place in bowl and cover with plastic wrap to allow the pepper to steam. After 20 minutes, peel skin away and discard. Dice the pepper and mix together with the other vegetables.

> Wild rice or "water grass" is native to the Minnesota area of the U.S. It is the only rice that sprouts, and it is beneficial to the nervous system, cleanses the body of toxins, soothes the stomach, and strengthens the spleen and pancreas.

Cumin Hemp Vinaigrette

     2 tablespoons rice wine vinegar

     1 tablespoon agave nectar (see Glossary)

     2 tablespoons ground cumin

    ^{1}/$_2$ cup hempseed oil

      salt and pepper to taste

→

Combine rice wine vinegar, agave nectar, and cumin in a blender. With the blender on a low speed, add the hempseed oil and blend until it begins to emulsify.

Add salt and pepper to taste.

To serve, mix the wild rice with the diced vegetables. Generously mix in the vinaigrette. Serve at room temperature.

Salad of Green Grapes, Dates, Lychee Nuts, Walnuts, & Hempnuts

SERVES 6

2 cups seedless green grapes, cut in halves
1 cup pitted organic dates, cut in halves
1 cup lychee nuts, cut in halves
1 cup raw walnuts, chopped
1/4 cup hempnuts
3–4 tablespoons hempseed oil

Mix together all ingredients and serve at room temperature.

Dressers

*T*his section could have been called "vinaigrettes and sauces," but again, as you choose these items, you will most definitely be "dressing" your dishes. Here we had some of the most fun, given the genuine worldly nature of hempseed oil and its possibilities. We'll take you from classic Caesar interpretations to French balsamic traditions, and introduce you to the world of Mexican mole and Indian curries. You can experiment with Japanese miso, Chinese hoisin, and Caribbean sambals, or hunker down for a home-style American seafood cookout with our Lobster and Shrimp Infused Hempseed Oils. The most distinctive dresser comes from Antonio Martinez, our line cook, who uses his grandmother's ancient recipe from central Mexico to slowly cook the mole. Some chefs have called Antonio's Hempnut Mole Sauce the best in New York City. The most popular recipe is our Hemp Miso Dressing, which will be available retail later this year.

Banana Sambal

YIELDS 2^1/4 CUPS

    2 tablespoons chili garlic sauce
    1 cup ketchup
    2 medium bananas
    2 tablespoons hempseed oil

Place all ingredients in a food processor and blend together until smooth.

Cilantro-Tangerine Hempnut Vinaigrette

YIELDS 2^1/4 CUPS

    ^{1}/2 cup tangerines with juice
    ^{1}/4 cup hempnuts
    2 tablespoons Dijon mustard
    ^{1}/4 cup rice wine vinegar
    1 teaspoon garlic, minced
    3 teaspoons shallots, minced
    ^{1}/2 cup peanut oil
    ^{1}/4 cup cilantro, chopped
    3 tablespoons mint, chopped

Mix all ingredients except the cilantro, mint, and oil in a blender until smooth. With the blender on a low speed, slowly add oil and blend until emulsified. Finish by adding the chopped cilantro and mint.

Apricot Hempseed Oil Vinaigrette

YIELDS 1^1/4 CUPS

^{1}/4 cup rehydrated apricots
^{1}/2 cup rice wine vinegar
2 tablespoons mirin (see Glossary)
1 tablespoon Dijon mustard
^{1}/4 cup hempseed oil
salt and pepper to taste
1 teaspoon garlic, minced

Place the apricots, vinegar, mirin, and Dijon mustard in a blender and blend until smooth. With the blender on a slow speed, add the hempseed oil and blend until emulsified. Add garlic and salt and pepper to taste.

Red Wine-Shallot Hempseed Oil Vinaigrette

YIELDS 1^1/2 CUPS

^{1}/2 cup red wine vinegar
2 shallots, peeled and minced
1 garlic clove, minced
1 tablespoon Dijon mustard
1 teaspoon herbs de Provence (see Glossary)
^{1}/2 cup hempseed oil
^{1}/4 cup extra virgin olive oil
1 teaspoon raw cane sugar (see Glossary)
salt and pepper to taste

Mix the vinegar, shallots, garlic, Dijon mustard, and herbs de Provence in a large mixing bowl.

Whisk ingredients until combined. Slowly add the hempseed and olive oils and whisk until emulsified.

Add sugar and salt and pepper to taste.

Curry Hempseed Oil Vinaigrette

Yields 1 cup

> 1 small red onion
> 1 medium Granny Smith apple, diced
> 1 tablespoon butter
> 1 teaspoon turmeric
> 2 tablespoons Madras curry (see Glossary)
> 1 teaspoon Dijon mustard
> juice of 2 lemons
> $^1/_4$ cup hempseed oil
> $^1/_2$ cup vegetable oil
> 1 teaspoon honey
> salt and pepper to taste

Peel and dice the onion and apple. Melt the butter in a skillet and sweat the onion and apple over medium-low heat for 5 to 6 minutes. Add the turmeric and curry and sauté for approximately 3 minutes.

Blend together the Dijon mustard and lemon juice in a blender or food processor. Slowly add hempseed oil and vegetable oil and blend until emulsified.

Add the onion-apple-curry mixture to blender. Add honey and blend together thoroughly. Season with salt and pepper to taste.

Hemp paper can be recycled ten times, as opposed to three times for most pulp-based paper.

Dried Shiitake Vinaigrette

YIELDS 1 CUP

2 egg yolks
1/2 clove garlic
1 teaspoon Dijon mustard
1/4 cup hempseed oil
1/4 cup peanut oil
1/4 cup dried shiitake mushrooms
2 cups water reserved from rehydration of mushrooms
juice of 1 lemon
2 tablespoons rice wine vinegar
salt and pepper to taste

Separate two eggs and place the yolks in a metal bowl. Add garlic and Dijon mustard and slowly whisk in hempseed oil and peanut oil. The oil should be added to the yolk mixture in a very slow stream. Be careful not to add the oil to fast or the aioli will separate.

Soak the dried shiitake mushrooms for 1 hour. Remove and discard the stems. (The stems are too hard and do not puree well.)

Place the mushrooms back in the water they were soaking in and blend the water and mushrooms to make a puree. Slowly pour the mushroom puree into the aioli base.

Add the lemon juice and rice vinegar. Season with salt and pepper to taste. Refrigerate.

Hempnut Watercress-Avocado Dressing

YIELDS 1 1/2 CUPS

1/4 cup fresh coriander, chopped
2 tablespoons watercress, chopped
2 tablespoons walnuts, chopped
3 tablespoons fresh-squeezed lime juice
1/2 avocado, chopped
1/2 teaspoon salt
1 tablespoon honey or maple syrup
1/2 teaspoon dry mustard
1/4 teaspoon paprika
1/3 cup hempseed oil

Combine all ingredients except the oil in a blender and blend until smooth. With the blender on a low speed, gradually add the oil and blend until emulsified. The mixture should be smooth and thick.

Tahini-Lime Hempnut Dressing

YIELDS 1 1/8 CUPS

1/2 cup tahini (see Glossary)
1 1/2 tablespoons honey or maple syrup
1 tablespoon fresh-squeezed lime juice
1 1/2 tablespoons rice vinegar
1/4 teaspoon salt
1/4 cup hempseed oil
2 tablespoons hempnuts

Mix all ingredients except the oil in a blender until smooth. With the blender on a low speed, slowly add the oil and blend until emulsified.

Hempnut Caesar Dressing

YIELDS 2 CUPS

> 1 egg yolk
> juice of 1 lemon
> $1/2$ cup extra virgin olive oil
> $1/4$ cup hempseed oil
> $1/2$ tube anchovy paste or 3 salt-packed anchovy filets (optional)
> $1/2$ cup parmesan, grated
> 2 tablespoons Worcestershire sauce
> 2 large garlic cloves
> 1 tablespoon Dijon mustard
> 2 tablespoons hempnuts
> salt to taste
> Tabasco to taste

Place the egg yolk and lemon juice in a blender. With the blender on medium, slowly add the olive and hempseed oils and blend until thick. Add the remainder of the ingredients and blend until completely mixed. Refrigerate.

Tofu Hemp Hoisin Vinaigrette

YIELDS $2^{1}/4$ CUPS

> 8 ounce package soft tofu
> $1/4$ cup hoisin sauce (see Glossary)
> $1/2$ cup rice wine vinegar
> $1/4$ cup water
> salt and pepper to taste
> $1/4$ cup hempseed oil

Blend the tofu, hoisin sauce, vinegar, water, and salt and pepper until smooth. Gradually add the hempseed oil and blend until combined.

Grapefruit Hemp Citronette

YIELDS 1$\frac{1}{2}$ CUPS

> 1 garlic clove, chopped
> 1 small shallot, chopped
> $\frac{1}{2}$ cup fresh-squeezed grapefruit juice
> $\frac{1}{4}$ cup hempseed oil
> $\frac{1}{2}$ cup grapeseed oil
> salt and pepper to taste

Blend the garlic, shallot, and grapefruit juice in a blender until smooth. With the blender on a slow speed, gradually add the hempseed and grapeseed oils and blend until emulsified. Add salt and pepper to taste.

Orange-Ginger Hemp Vinaigrette

YIELDS 1$\frac{1}{4}$ CUPS

> 1-inch piece fresh ginger, grated
> 2 tablespoons fresh-squeezed lime juice
> 2 tablespoons soy sauce
> $\frac{1}{2}$ cup fresh-squeezed orange juice
> $\frac{1}{4}$ cup hempseed oil
> $\frac{1}{4}$ cup vegetable oil

Mix the grated ginger and lime juice in a blender or a metal bowl. Allow mixture to sit for at least 30 minutes to allow the flavors to fuse together.

Whisk in the soy sauce and orange juice. Gradually add the hempseed and vegetable oils. Whisk briskly before using.

Fig Hemp Balsamic Vinaigrette

YIELDS 1 1/3 CUPS

> 4 fresh figs, tops clipped and cut into chunks
> 1/3 cup aged balsamic vinegar
> 1 garlic clove
> 1 tablespoon Dijon mustard
> 1/2 cup hempseed oil
> 1/4 cup olive oil
> 1/2 teaspoon fresh thyme
> salt and pepper to taste

Blend the figs, balsamic vinegar, garlic, and Dijon mustard in a blender until smooth. With the blender on a low speed, gradually add the hempseed and olive oils and blend until emulsified. Add the thyme and salt and pepper to taste.

Hemp Miso Dressing

YIELDS 2 1/2 –2 3/4 CUPS

> 1 cup shiro miso paste (see Glossary)
> 1/4 cup soy sauce
> 1/2 cup rice wine vinegar
> 1/2 cup hempseed oil
> 1/4 –1/2 cup peanut oil

Blend the miso paste, soy sauce, and rice wine vinegar in a blender on high speed. Turn the blender to a low speed and slowly add the hempseed oil.

Once incorporated, adjust to desired thickness by adding peanut oil.

Mojo Vinaigrette

YIELDS 2¹/4 CUPS

> 1 cup sour orange juice or ¹/3 cup lime juice and ²/3 cup orange juice
> 2 garlic cloves
> 1 tablespoon Dijon mustard
> ¹/2 cup hempseed oil
> ¹/2 cup olive oil
> 1 tablespoon fresh oregano
> ¹/2 tablespoon ground cumin
> 1 tablespoon raw cane sugar (see Glossary)
> salt and pepper to taste

Whisk the juice, garlic, and Dijon mustard in a stainless steel bowl until combined. Add the hempseed and olive oils gradually and whisk until emulsified. Add the oregano, cumin, and sugar and whisk until combined. Add salt and pepper to taste.

Agave-Whole Grain Mustard Vinaigrette

YIELDS 1¹/2 CUPS

> ¹/2 cup apple cider vinegar
> 2 tablespoons agave nectar (see Glossary)
> 2 tablespoons whole grain mustard
> ¹/3 cup hempseed oil
> ¹/3 cup olive oil
> 1 teaspoon dried thyme
> salt and pepper to taste

Whisk the vinegar, agave nectar, and whole grain mustard in a stainless steel bowl until combined. Gradually add the hempseed and olive oils and whisk until emulsified. Add the thyme and salt and pepper to taste.

Golden Raisin Hemp Dressing

<small>YIELDS 1^1/$_2$ CUPS</small>

^{1}/$_2$ cup golden raisins
1 teaspoon garlic, minced
1 tablespoon Dijon mustard
juice of 1 lemon
^{1}/$_3$ cup apple cider vinegar
^{1}/$_4$ cup hempseed oil
^{1}/$_4$ cup olive oil
salt and pepper to taste

Blend the raisins, garlic, Dijon mustard, lemon juice, and vinegar in a blender. With the blender on a low speed, slowly add the hempseed and olive oils and blend until emulsified. Add salt and pepper to taste.

Caper-Jalapeño Sauce

<small>YIELDS 1^2/$_3$ CUPS</small>

1 egg yolk
1 teaspoon Dijon mustard
2 tablespoons fresh-squeezed lime juice
^{2}/$_3$ cup olive oil
^{1}/$_3$ cup hempseed oil
1 tablespoon jalapeño peppers, chopped
3 tablespoons capers
1 teaspoon agave nectar (see Glossary)
salt and pepper to taste

Mix the egg yolk, Dijon mustard, and lime juice in a stainless steel bowl. Whisk until all ingredients are combined.

Gradually add the olive and hempseed oils and whisk until emulsified. The consistency will be that of a mayonnaise. Mix in the jalapeño, capers, and agave nectar. Add salt and pepper to taste.

Hemp Sambal Mentah

Yields 2¹/₂ cups

> 7 shallots, peeled and finely sliced
> 2 garlic cloves
> 7 small green-bird chilies (see Glossary), seeded and finely chopped
> 2 lime leaves (see Glossary), finely sliced
> 2 lemon grass stalks (see Glossary), very finely sliced
> ¹/₂ teaspoon shrimp paste
> 1 tablespoon fresh-squeezed lime juice
> ¹/₄ cup hempseed oil
> salt and pepper to taste

Combine all ingredients in a stainless steel bowl and mix well with a wooden spoon.

Add salt and pepper to taste. Use as a condiment for any seafood dish. Store covered in a sealed container for up to 2 weeks.

Spicy Hemp Dipping Sauce

Yields ³/₄ cups

> 1 egg yolk
> 1 teaspoon fresh-squeezed lime juice
> ¹/₂ cup hempseed oil
> ¹/₂ teaspoon cayenne pepper
> ¹/₂ teaspoon red chili flakes
> 1 teaspoon raw cane sugar (see Glossary)
> salt and pepper to taste

Mix the egg yolk and lime juice in a stainless steel bowl.

Gradually add the hempseed oil and whisk until emulsified. The consistency will be that of a mayonnaise. Mix in the cayenne pepper, chili flakes, and sugar. Add salt and pepper to taste. Refrigerate until ready to serve.

Cucumber Sauce

YIELDS 1¹/2 CUPS

     1 egg yolk
     1 garlic clove, chopped
     1/4 cup hempseed oil
     1/4 cup peanut oil
     1 teaspoon Dijon mustard
     1/4 cup rice vinegar
     1/2 cucumber
     pinch of cayenne
     1/2 teaspoon cumin
     salt and pepper to taste

Place the egg yolk in a metal bowl. Add the garlic and slowly whisk in the hempseed and peanut oils. The oil should be added to the yolk mixture in a very slow stream. Be careful not to add the oil too fast or the aioli will separate.

Blend the Dijon mustard, rice vinegar, and unpeeled washed cucumber. Puree until cucumber is completely liquefied. Stir slowly into the aioli.

Add the cayenne and cumin. Season with salt and pepper to taste. Refrigerate until ready to serve.

In *Fats that Heal, Fats that Kill,* author Eudo Erasmus states that because of the ideal ratio of essential fatty acids (3:1 of omega-6 to omega-3), hempseed oil may be nature's most perfectly balanced oil. (Alive Books, Burnaby, B.C., 1993)

Oregano Hemp Aioli

YIELDS 3/4 CUPS

> 1 egg yolk
> 1 garlic clove, chopped
> 1/4 cup hempseed oil
> 1/4 cup peanut oil
> 1 teaspoon Dijon mustard
> 1 teaspoon fresh-squeezed lemon juice
> 1 bunch fresh oregano
> salt and pepper to taste

Place the egg yolk in a metal bowl. Add the garlic and slowly whisk in the hempseed and peanut oils. The oil should be added to the yolk mixture in a very slow stream. Be careful not to add the oil too fast or the aioli will separate. Whisk in the Dijon mustard and lemon juice.

Pull the leaves from the sprigs of oregano. (It is important to chop fresh herbs with a sharp knife so they don't bruise or leave the flavor on the cutting board and not in the vinaigrette.)

Add the chopped oregano and season with salt and pepper to taste. If the aioli is too thick whisk in a tablespoon of water. Refrigerate until ready to serve.

Orange Hemp Aioli

YIELDS 2 3/4 CUPS

> 2 egg yolks
> 1/2 cup hempseed oil
> 1 1/2 cups extra virgin olive oil
> 2 tablespoons orange zest
> 2 tablespoons fresh-squeezed lime juice
> 4 tablespoons cilantro, finely chopped
> salt and pepper to taste

Place the egg yolks in a metal bowl. Add garlic and slowly whisk in hempseed and olive oils. The oils should be added to the yolk mixture in a very slow stream. Be careful not to add the oil too fast or the aioli will separate. Whisk in the orange zest, lime juice, and chopped cilantro. Add salt and pepper to taste. Refrigerate until ready to serve.

Rosemary Aioli

YIELDS 1$^1/_2$ CUPS

> 2 egg yolks
> 1 garlic clove, chopped
> $^1/_2$ cup hempseed oil
> $^1/_4$ cup extra virgin olive oil
> $^1/_4$ cup vegetable oil
> $^1/_2$ teaspoon Dijon mustard
> 1 teaspoon fresh-squeezed lemon juice
> 1 bunch rosemary
> salt and pepper to taste

Place the egg yolks in a metal bowl. Add the garlic and slowly whisk in the hempseed, olive, and vegetable oils. The oils should be added to the yolk mixture in a very slow stream. Be careful not to add the oil too fast or the aioli will separate. Whisk in the Dijon mustard and lemon juice.

Pull the leaves from the sprigs of rosemary. (It is important to chop fresh herbs with a sharp knife so they don't bruise or leave the flavor on the cutting board and not in the vinaigrette.)

Add the chopped rosemary and season with salt and pepper to taste. If the consistency of the aioli is too thick whisk in a tablespoon of water. Refrigerate until ready to serve.

Southwestern Aioli

YIELDS 1 1/2 CUPS

2 egg yolks
1 garlic clove, chopped
1/2 cup hempseed oil
1/4 cup vegetable oil
juice of 2 limes
1 tablespoon tomato paste
1/2 teaspoon cayenne pepper
1/2 teaspoon black pepper
3 tablespoons chili powder
1 teaspoon cumin

Place the egg yolks in a metal bowl. Add the garlic and slowly whisk in hempseed and vegetable oils. The oils should be added to the yolk mixture in a very slow stream. Be careful not to add the oil too fast or the aioli will separate. Whisk in the lime juice and tomato paste. Season with cayenne pepper, black pepper, cumin, and chili powder. Refrigerate until ready to serve.

Variations

Substitute one chipotle pepper for cayenne pepper.
Add chopped cilantro.
Add chunks of avocado.

Until about 1800, hempseed oil was the most-used lighting oil in America and the world.

Lemon-Ginger Hemp Aioli

YIELDS 1³/4 CUPS

       2 egg yolks
   1/2 cup hempseed oil
   1/2 cup extra virgin olive oil
   1/4 cup fresh-squeezed lemon juice
     1 tablespoon lemon zest
     1 tablespoon fresh ginger, minced
   1/2 teaspoon dried ginger powder
     1 teaspoon dried sage
       salt and pepper to taste

Place the egg yolks in a metal bowl. Add garlic and slowly whisk in hempseed and olive oils. The oils should be added to the yolk mixture in a very slow stream. Be careful not to add the oil too fast or the aioli will separate. Mix in the lemon juice and zest. Mix in the fresh ginger and ginger powder. Add the sage and salt and pepper to taste. Refrigerate until ready to serve.

Hempnut Cashew-Cilantro Pesto

YIELDS 2 CUPS

   1/4 cup hempnuts
   1/4 cup cashews
     4 bunches fresh cilantro
   1/4 cup parmesan
   1/4 cup hempseed oil
   1/4 cup extra virgin olive oil
     1 small poblano pepper, seeded
       salt and pepper to taste

Blend all ingredients in a blender or food processor until smooth. Add salt and pepper to taste.

Antonio's Hempnut Mole Sauce

Makes 2 pounds or 12 cups

1 bread roll, diced
1 tortilla, cut in triangles
1/2 cup coconut oil or other high-temperature frying oil
1/2 gallon water
2 tablespoons guajillo peppers (see Glossary)
2 tablespoons almonds, chopped
3 tablespoons sesame seeds
3 tablespoons unsalted peanuts, chopped
3 tablespoons hempnuts
3 tablespoons walnuts, chopped
2 tablespoons raisins
7 tablespoons abuelita chocolate (see Glossary)
10 tablespoons ground cumin
5–8 spice cloves
1/2 tablespoon whole black peppercorns
1 cup mole base (see Glossary)

Deep-fry the roll and tortilla in the oil until golden and crispy.

Bring the water to a boil. Deseed the peppers and tear into strips.

Add all ingredients except the mole base to the boiling water.

Boil the ingredients until the peppers are soft. Blend the mixture in batches in a blender, adding little amounts of mole base to each batch.

Return to the pot and simmer over a low flame for 1 hour to allow the flavors to absorb and meld together. Cool and refrigerate for up to a week.

Hemp Marinara

YIELD 1$\frac{1}{3}$ CUPS

 2 tablespoons olive oil
 1 small white onion, diced
 2 garlic cloves, minced
 1 tablespoon red chili flakes
 1 bay leaf
 $\frac{1}{2}$ cup hempnuts
 10 ripe plum tomatoes, peeled and chopped
 1 teaspoon tomato paste
 $\frac{1}{2}$ cup fresh basil, chopped
 2 cups water
 1 tablespoon raw cane sugar (see Glossary)
 $\frac{1}{4}$ cup hempseed oil
 salt and pepper to taste

Heat the olive oil in a pot. Add the onion, garlic, chili flakes, and bay leaf. Sauté for 3 minutes, or until translucent and beginning to turn golden.

Add the hempnuts, tomatoes, tomato paste, $\frac{1}{4}$ cup of basil, and 1 cup of water. Cook over medium heat for 10 minutes. Add the second cup water, reduce to medium-low heat, and cook for another 15 minutes.

Add the sugar and hempseed oil and cook for 5 minutes more. Do not allow to boil. Add the remaining $\frac{1}{4}$ cup of basil. Use a hand-held mixer to blend the sauce to a smooth puree, adding a little water if necessary.

Add salt and pepper to taste. Serve.

Infused Hempseed Oils

Curry Oil

YIELDS 1 CUP

> 3 tablespoons Madras curry powder (see Glossary)
> 2 teaspoons turmeric powder
> 1 cup hempseed oil
> 1 bay leaf
> salt and pepper to taste

Let ingredients simmer in pan for five minutes. Allow to steep for 20 minutes. Remove bay leaf. Strain.

Habanero Oil

YIELDS 2¹/2 CUPS

> 1 habanero chili, finely diced
> 1 cup hempseed oil
> 1¹/2 cups extra virgin olive oil
> salt and pepper to taste

Chop the habanero chili into finely diced pieces. Be sure to wear latex gloves when using chilies (especially the habanero). Do not touch your eyes or lips— or else! Mix the oils and add the peppers to the mixture. Season with a little salt and pepper. Stir occasionally. This oil takes time to mature. The heat of the pepper will incorporate into the oils over time. It will need at least one day for the flavors to absorb and meld together.

Lobster or Shrimp Oil

YIELDS 2 CUPS

2 uncooked lobster bodies *or* 1 cup uncooked shrimp shells
1 cup grapeseed oil
1 teaspoon tomato paste
2 garlic cloves
1 teaspoon coriander seeds
  salt and pepper to taste
1 tablespoon brandy
1 cup hempseed oil

If using lobster, clean the lobster bodies well. Lift the shell from the thorax and remove the sack that is right behind the eyes. This sack is the stomach. It will bring a bitter flavor to the oil. Scrape away the spongy textured tissue found on both sides of the thorax. These are the lungs and will also lend an undesirable taste.

Chop each lobster carcass into at least 8 pieces. If you are using the shrimp shells start from this point. Add 2 tablespoons of the grapeseed oil to a hot smoking pan. Add the shellfish. The pan should sizzle. Shells will turn a bright red color and then start to brown. Turn the heat down to medium and add the tomato paste, garlic cloves, and coriander seeds. Season with salt and pepper to taste. Watch carefully for any ingredients that start to burn. Pull the pan off the burner immediately if this happens.

This combination will become very aromatic. Pull the pan off the burner and pour in the brandy. Carefully return the pan to the burner. The brandy may ignite and flame up. This is called a flambé. It will only burn for a few seconds. Let the brandy evaporate completely, then add the rest of the grapeseed and hempseed oils.

Turn the stove down to a low heat. Do not allow the oil to simmer. The oil should not exceed 160°F. Cook for an additional 10 minutes. Pull the pan off the burner and let it steep for another 15 minutes.

Strain the oil through a fine sieve. Emulsify in blender and add more salt and pepper if needed. This oil may separate over a little time. It may be necessary to re-emulsify oil before using. Store in the refrigerator for up to 2 weeks.

Mediterranean Herb Oil

YIELDS 2 CUPS

1 rosemary sprig
1 thyme sprig
1 bay leaf
1 teaspoon fennel seed
5 black peppercorns
3 garlic cloves
2 cups hempseed oil

Let all the ingredients simmer in a pan until garlic is golden brown and soft. Allow to steep for 20 minutes. Remove bay leaf, peppercorns, and thyme sprig. Place the remaining mixture in blender and puree. Strain through fine sieve.

Stellar Starters

*T*his chapter best represents the creative spirit and mission statement of The Galaxy Global Eatery by focusing on our favorite food source—vegetables. In this section and the next, Quasars, we present traditional recipes, with hemp, that can be the perfect beginning to any party or event, be it an intimate dinner with friends or the biggest cocktail party of the year. Korean Seitan Lettuce Wraps, Japanese Hempura, and Ecuadorian Sweet Potato-Quinoa Soufflé exemplify the global diversity of recipes you can prepare. For the flavor of the East Coast of Africa, serve Chef Kris's Warm Spicy African Nut Mix with Fruit and show The Galaxy Global Eatery at its best. Edamame Cakes with Mango-Hot Pepper Aioli will be a winner at any gathering. Hempnut-crusted grains and soybeans are an exciting example of the marriage of the exquisite seed with your favorite carbo-hydrates. Minted Melon Norimaki rolls are true crowd-pleasers, as are the Pumpkin Hempanadas. Why start, if stellar it is not?

Pumpkin Hempanadas

with Black Pumpkin Seed Oil Dipping Sauce & Shiitake Mushroom Salad

SERVES 6

Pumpkin Hempanadas

>   1 2-pound pumpkin, peeled, seeded, and cut into chunks
>   2 tablespoons olive oil
>   3 ears corn
>   3 garlic cloves, minced
>   1/2 cup hempnuts
>   3 tablespoons hempseed oil
>   3 tablespoons fresh sage, chopped
>   salt and pepper to taste
>   1 bunch scallions, thinly sliced
>   30 pieces gyoza dumpling wrappers (see Glossary)
>   2 cups clarified butter (see Glossary)

Preheat oven to 450°F.

Toss the pumpkin with the olive oil, place on a cookie sheet, and roast in the oven for 45 minutes, or until tender and fragrant. Set aside to cool.

Put a pot of water to boil. Add the corn and boil until bright yellow and tender (about 5–8 minutes). Transfer to a grill and roast until golden on all sides. Strip off the kernels and set them aside.

Blend the pumpkin to a puree in a food processor or blender, then add the garlic, hempnuts, hempseed oil, and fresh sage. Add salt and pepper to taste.

Mix in the corn kernels and scallions with a spatula.

Lay out the gyoza skins on a large table or counter top.

Spoon 1 heaping tablespoon of the mixture in the middle of each dumpling wrapper. Use your fingers and a cup of water to moisten the edges of the wrappers. Fold the dumpling wrappers in half to form half moons. Seal them closed by pressing the edges together. Heat the butter in a large sauté pan. Place the hempanadas side by side and fry until golden brown. Transfer to paper towels to absorb the oil. Set aside.

→

Black Pumpkin Seed Oil Dipping Sauce

1/4 cup rice wine vinegar

1 teaspoon Dijon mustard

1 garlic clove

1/2 cup Austrian black pumpkin seed oil

salt and pepper to taste

Blend together the rice wine vinegar, Dijon mustard, and garlic until smooth. Add the pumpkin seed oil gradually until an emulsion forms. Season with salt and pepper to taste. Set aside.

Shiitake Mushroom Salad

12 ounces mustard greens, washed, chopped, and blanched

24 pieces rehydrated shiitake mushrooms

1/4 cup soy sauce

Garnish: 1 cup finely grated daikon radish

1 cup finely grated carrot

Mix the mustard greens, shiitake mushrooms, and soy sauce in a bowl. Grate the daikon and carrot in long spaghetti-thin strips with a mandolin (see Glossary).

To serve, place the Shiitake Mushroom Salad on one side of a large plate. Garnish with the daikon and carrot. Place the Pumpkin Hempanadas next to the salad. Serve the Black Pumpkin Seed Oil Dipping Sauce in a ramekin.

Warm Spicy African Nut Mix with Fruits

SERVES 6

2 tablespoons olive oil
2 tablespoons hempseed oil
1/2 cup dried dates, pitted
1/3 cup dried apricots
1/2 cup raw almonds
1/2 cup raw cashews
1/2 cup raw macadamia nuts, halved
1/2 cup raw pecans, halved
    finely grated zest of one lemon or lime
2–3 tablespoons coriander leaves
1 red chili, deseeded and finely chopped
    salt and pepper to taste

Warm the olive and hempseed oils in a large frying pan over medium heat.

Add all the dried fruit and nuts and toss until the apricots and nuts begin to color. Remove from the heat and add the lemon or lime zest, coriander leaves, and chili. Mix thoroughly, season to taste, and serve warm from the pan in small bowls as a snack.

Hemp's deep root system is very beneficial as it is effective in preventing erosion, cleaning the ground, providing a disease break, and helping soil structure by aerating the soil for future crops when grown in rotation with other crops.

Hempnut Mushroom Cakes
with Caper-Jalapeño Sauce

SERVES 4

Hempnut Mushroom Cakes

        5 portobello mushrooms
        1 teaspoon vegetable oil
        1 teaspoon thyme buds
        1 teaspoon garlic, chopped
      1/2 cup cheddar cheese, shredded
        2 eggs
           salt and pepper to taste
        2 cups panko bread crumbs (see Glossary)
        5 scallions, chopped
           unbleached white flour for dredging
        1 cup hempnuts
        4 tablespoons (1/2 stick) butter
        1 red pepper

Clean the mushrooms by removing gills. Heat the vegetable oil and sauté mushrooms for about 3 minutes. Allow to cool.

Puree the mushrooms in a food processor.

Mix the thyme buds, garlic, cheddar cheese, and 1 of the eggs in a bowl. Season with salt and pepper to taste. Add 1 cup of panko bread crumbs and incorporate. Add chopped scallions and mushroom mixture to the bowl. Divide the mixture into 8 parts and pat each into individual 2-inch cakes. Set out three bowls. Fill one with flour, one with the second egg, whisked, and another with the rest of the panko bread crumbs and the hempnuts mixed together. Dredge the cakes by dipping each one first in flour, then in egg, then in the bread crumb-hempnut mixture. The hempnuts should easily adhere to the cake due to the stickiness of the flour-egg combination.

Heat the butter in a sauté pan over medium-high heat. Add the cakes and fry until brown (about 3 minutes per side).

Cut the red pepper in half and deseed. Discard the white membrane and dice into very small pieces. Set aside.

Caper-Jalapeño Sauce

    2 egg yolks
    1 garlic clove
    $1/2$ cup peanut oil
    $1/2$ cup hempseed oil
    1 tablespoon fresh-squeezed lime juice
    1 jalapeño, deseeded and chopped
    $1/2$ cup capers, chopped
    $1/2$ cup sour cream
    salt and pepper to taste

Place the 2 egg yolks in a metal bowl. Add garlic and slowly whisk in the peanut and hempseed oils. The oil should be added to the yolk mixture in a slow stream. Be careful not to add the oil too fast or the sauce will separate.

Mix the lime juice, jalapeño, and capers together.

Fold in the sour cream and season with salt and pepper to taste.

To serve, ladle the Caper-Jalapeño Sauce onto the center of a serving plate and place the Hempnut Mushroom Cakes on top. Sprinkle the diced red pepper like confetti around the plate.

Green Papaya Spring Rolls
with *Spicy Hemp Dipping Sauce*

SERVES 4

Green Papaya Spring Rolls

> 1 medium green papaya, shredded
> 1 medium Granny Smith apple, shredded
> 1 carrot, shredded
> 2 scallions, diced
> 2 tablespoons garam masala powder (see Glossary)
> 1/4 cup hempnuts
> 1 tablespoon salt
> 8 spring roll wrappers (see Glossary)
> coconut oil or other high-temperature frying oil

Peel the green papaya and remove its seeds. Using a home mandolin (see Glossary), cut the papaya into spaghetti-thin strips. Peel the apple and carrot and cut into spaghetti-thin strips. Dice the scallion and combine with the rest. Add garam masala, hempnuts, and salt.

Divide the mixture into 8 parts. Take 1 portion and place it evenly along one side of a spring roll wrapper. Roll up the spring roll, and tucking in the sides as it is rolled. Moisten the end with water to create a seal. Set aside and repeat until all are used. Heat the coconut oil and place the spring rolls in the hot oil. Turn the rolls every 15 seconds. Cook until crispy and golden brown. Cut at a bias. Set aside.

→

Green papaya is high in the proteolytic digestive enzyme papain. It helps to digest proteins in the diet and cleanse the body of old, accumulated protein matter. Because of this, green papaya is excellent to use while fasting and for bowel cleansing programs. Papaya also contains arganine, essential for male fertility and carpaine, an enzyme for heart health. Carpaine also has an anti-bacterial effect.

Spicy Hemp Dipping Sauce

      2 Thai chili peppers (see Glossary), deseeded
      3 tablespoons mirin (see Glossary)
      1 tablespoon fresh-squeezed lime juice
      1 small garlic clove, diced
      2 tablespoons hempseed oil
        salt and pepper to taste

Carefully dice the Thai chili pepper and place in metal bowl. Add mirin, lime juice, and garlic. Whisk in hempseed oil and season with salt and pepper.

Garnish

      1 medium Granny Smith apple
      1 teaspoon butter
      8 ounces mesclun greens

Slice off the very top and bottom, and then cut the Granny Smith apple cross-wise into 4 slices, leaving the skin on. Use an apple corer or a knife to remove the core, leaving a perfect circular hole in the center. Place a sauté pan over medium heat and add the butter. Once the butter is hot, add the apple slices. Cook for 2 minutes on each side, or until golden brown. Set aside.

To serve, dress the mesclun greens with a little Spicy Hemp Dipping Sauce and thread the mesclun through the hole in the sautéed apple. Place the apple and mesclun at 12 o'clock on a serving plate. Lean the Green Papaya Spring Rolls against the cored apple. Serve remaining dipping sauce in a ramekin on the side.

Hemp Polenta
with Olive Hemp Spread

SERVES 4

Hemp Polenta

> 4 cups whole milk
> 1/4 cup butter
> 1 teaspoon salt
> 1/2 cup hemp flour
> 1 1/2 cups cornmeal
> 1 tablespoon cumin
> 1 teaspoon red pepper flakes

Boil the milk and butter in a pot, then add the salt. Slowly add the hemp flour and cornmeal while stirring constantly. Add the cumin and pepper flakes. Allow to boil for 4 minutes. Remove from the heat and spread out 1-inch thick on a cookie sheet. Allow to cool.

Olive Hemp Spread

> 1/2 cup pitted olives (Kalamata or Nicoise)
> 1 garlic clove, chopped
> 1/2 teaspoon ground fennel seed
> 2 tablespoons hempseed oil
> 1 tablespoon fresh basil, chopped

Blend the pitted olives, garlic, fennel seed, and hempseed oil and puree to a paste.

Serve the Hemp Polenta in triangles, or another shape of your choice. Spread Olive Hemp Spread on one side. Place a pinch of chopped basil on top of each piece. This is a perfect appetizer or finger food.

Hemp-Crusted Chickpea & Corn Kofta
with Curry-Tamarind Sauce

SERVES 6

Hemp-Crusted Kofta

2 russet potatoes, peeled and diced

1 16-ounce can chickpeas

2 ears corn, kernels removed

2 tablespoons garam masala (see Glossary)

2 tablespoons fresh-squeezed lemon juice

1/4 cup unbleached white flour

2 tablespoons salt

1/4 teaspoon cayenne pepper

1/2 cup hempnuts

1 tablespoon butter or vegetable oil

Place diced potatoes in salted boiling water. Cook until tender, then coarsely mash. Puree half the can of chickpeas in a food processor. Combine with the rest of the whole chickpeas, the cooked potatoes, and corn kernels. Add the garam masala, lemon juice, flour, salt, and cayenne pepper to chickpea-potato mixture. Form into golf-sized balls and then roll in hempnuts.

Place a sauté pan over medium heat and add the butter. Place the hemp-crusted kofta in the pan and cook for approximately 4 minutes per side, or until golden brown.

Curry-Tamarind Sauce

1 tablespoon butter

1 medium red onion, diced

1 13.5-ounce can unsweetened coconut milk

2 tablespoons tamarind paste (see Glossary)

2 tablespoons curry powder (see Glossary)

1/2 teaspoon turmeric powder

1 tablespoon agave nectar (see Glossary) or honey

10 mint leaves

Heat the butter over medium heat and add the diced red onion. Cook for about 3 minutes. Add coconut milk, tamarind paste, curry, and turmeric. Cook until the coconut milk reduces by half. Add agave nectar and mint leaves and allow to steep for 20 seconds. Let sauce cool to room temperature. Blend all ingredients for 2 minutes and then strain through a fine mesh strainer.

To serve, ladle the Curry-Tamarind Sauce in the center of a serving plate and place the Hemp-Crusted Kofta over the sauce.

Batata Puree

Yields 2 cups

> 3/4 cup batata (white sweet potato)
> 4 garlic cloves
> 1 recipe Hemp Milk (page 4)
>   salt and pepper to taste
> 1 tablespoon agave nectar (see Glossary) or honey

Preheat oven to 400°F.

Prick the sweet potatoes with a fork and wrap them in foil. Roast in the oven until the potatoes are fork tender.

Place whole peeled garlic cloves in enough water to cover in a sauce pan. Let the water come to a boil. Repeat this 2 more times. This process removes the sharp, raw taste of the garlic. Set aside.

Once the potatoes are tender, remove the potatoes from their skins and combine with the Hemp Milk, poached garlic, and agave nectar or honey. Puree until velvety smooth. Season with salt and pepper to taste. Serve in a bowl.

Corn-Spinach Hemp Wontons
with Pineapple Chutney

MAKES 20 WONTONS

1 ear corn
1 tablespoon peanut oil
1/2 cup spinach, cleaned and deveined
1 teaspoon cumin
1/2 teaspoon cayenne pepper
2 tablespoons hempnuts
1/2 cup coconut milk
2 tablespoons hempseed oil
salt and pepper to taste
20 wonton wrappers
coconut oil or other high-temperature frying oil

Shuck one ear of corn and remove kernels from cob. Heat the peanut oil and sauté the spinach. Add corn kernels, cumin, cayenne pepper, hempnuts, and coconut milk. Lower the heat to a simmer and reduce the coconut milk until thick. Allow to cool. Add hempseed oil. Season with salt and pepper to taste.

Place 1 teaspoon of the corn-spinach filling in the center of each wonton wrapper. Moisten the outer edge of the wrapper with a little water. This enables the wonton to seal. Fold the wonton in half and seal all edges. Moisten the long ends and join them. Heat the coconut oil to 375°F in a large sauté pan. With enough oil to cover them, deep fry the wontons until golden brown. Set aside.

> Corn is alkaline-forming, improves appetite, and regulates digestion. Corn is good for the gums, teeth, and heart. A tea of its kernels helps with kidney disease.

Pineapple Chutney

       1 tablespoon peanut oil
       1 red onion
       1 garlic clove
1-inch piece ginger
       $^1/_2$ pineapple, chopped
       $^1/_4$ cup agave nectar (see Glossary) or honey
       $^3/_4$ cup rice wine vinegar
       1 mint sprig

Place peanut oil in a heated saucepan and sweat the red onion, garlic, and ginger until soft. Add the pineapple and cook for about 4 minutes. Add the agave nectar and rice wine vinegar and reduce by half over medium-low heat. Allow to chill.

To serve, ladle the Pineapple Chutney onto the center of a serving plate and stack the Corn-Spinach Hemp Wontons around it. Garnish with the mint sprig.

In the belief that the spirits of dead relatives visit every Christmas Eve, the Polish and Lithuanian people prepared them a soup of hempseeds called Semieniatka.—Kenneth Jones, *Nutritional and Medicinal Guide to Hemp Seed,* 1995

Edamame Cakes

with Mango-Hot Pepper Aioli

SERVES 6

Edamame Cakes

    4 garlic cloves

    4 shallots

    4 tablespoons hempseed oil

    1 pound edamame beans (see Glossary)

      salt and pepper to taste

      hemp flour for dredging

    2 eggs, beaten

    2 cups hempnuts

      coconut oil or other high-temperature frying oil

Dice the garlic and shallots and sweat over low heat in hempseed oil (about 2 minutes). Add the edamame beans and season with salt and pepper to taste. Place the mixture in a food processor and blend until chunky-smooth. Season again if necessary. Form into eighteen 2-ounce cylindrical cakes and set aside.

    In three separate bowls, place hemp flour, eggs, and hempnuts. First place the Edamame Cakes into flour, then eggs, and finally roll them in hempnuts. Fry the Edamame Cakes in a pan in 350°F coconut oil for about 2 minutes, until hempnuts are a light golden brown. Set aside.

Mango-Hot Pepper Aioli

    2 egg yolks

    2 teaspoons Dijon mustard

      juice of 2 lemons

    2 cups vegetable oil

    2 medium mangos

    2 teaspoons Korean Red Pepper Sauce (see Glossary)

Place egg yolks, Dijon mustard, and lemon juice in a stainless steel bowl. Whisk together and slowly drizzle in the vegetable oil. The mixture should thicken to the consistency of mayonnaise. Peel and dice one mango. Puree the other mango to

a smooth juice. Add the diced mango, mango puree, and red pepper sauce to the aioli and stir together.

Salad Fixings

      1 head red leaf lettuce

      1 head frissee leaf lettuce

To serve, place the Mango-Hot Pepper Aioli in the center of a serving plate. Mound the leaves of red lettuce around a smaller amount of frissee leaves in the center of the sauce. Place 3 Edamame Cakes in the sauce around the lettuce.

Minted Melon Norimaki
with Mint Coulis Sauce

SERVES 4

     2 tablespoons unsalted butter

     1 large shallot, minced

     2 cups jasmine rice

     4 cups unsweetened coconut milk

$1/2$ cup mirin (see Glossary)

     1 piece lemon grass (see Glossary), split down the middle

     4 lime leaves (see Glossary) *or* the zest of 3 limes

    10 shiso leaves, finely chopped chiffonade (see Glossary)

$1/2$ cantaloupe melon

$1/2$ honeydew melon

     4 sheets of nori sushi paper

$1/4$ cup toasted hempnuts

Heat the butter in a medium size pan and sauté the shallot until translucent (approximately 2–4 minutes). Add the rice and coat with the shallot and butter mix.

    Add the coconut milk, mirin, lemon grass, and lime leaves. Cover and cook on low heat until rice is done (about 14–20 minutes). Allow to cool and set aside.

Peel the outer skin and remove the seeds from both the cantaloupe and honeydew melons. Slice the melons thin and long into 4-inch long spaghetti strips. Cut the mint leaves into small strips.

Assemble the rolls by placing 1 dry nori sheet on a bamboo rolling mat. (Use a paper towel if you don't have one.) Divide the rice mixture into 4 equal parts and use your fingers to spread 1 portion of rice evenly over the nori sheet, leaving a 1/2-inch border on all sides. Repeat for each nori sheet.

Combine the honeydew and cantaloupe slices and divide into 4 portions. Take 1 portion and place it in an even row at the closest end of the rice-covered nori sheet, on top of the rice. Place a small amount of the mint on top of the melon.

Take the side of the nori sheet closest to you and begin rolling it away from you, using your fingers to control the evenness. If you are using a paper towel, remove it as you go. The bamboo rolling mat will allow you to roll into a firmer shape. Once the sheet is rolled to the point where it will be sealed, wet the very end, where you have left a 1/2-inch border, with a bit of water and seal it. The water allows the top of the sheet to stick to the outside of the completed roll.

Mint Coulis Sauce

> 1/2 cup sugar
> 1/4 cup water
> 10–14 mint leaves
> 1 tablespoon clear gelatin (dissolved in 2 tablespoons cool water)

Prepare a simple syrup by bringing the sugar and water to a boil. Add the mint, thicken with the dissolved gelatin, strain, and set aside.

To serve, cut each Minted Melon Norimaki roll into 6 pieces, arrange them on a serving plate, and top with the Mint Coulis Sauce. Sprinkle with toasted hemp-nuts and serve.

Flaky Hempnut Scallion Pancakes
with Dried Fruit Chutney, Vegetable Pâté, & Green Chili Jelly

SERVES 6

Hempnut Scallion Pancakes

3 cups cake flour

1/4 cup unbleached white flour

1/4 cup hemp flour

1 teaspoon salt

2 tablespoons corn oil

13/4 cups boiling water

1/4 cup or more unbleached white flour for kneading

1 cup scallion greens, minced

1/4 cup sesame oil

3/4 cup coconut oil

Stir the cake, white, and hemp flours with the salt in a mixing bowl. Add the corn oil and boiling water and stir until a rough dough forms. If the dough is too soft, knead in about 1/4 cup more flour. Turn the dough out onto a lightly floured surface and knead for 5 minutes, until smooth. Wrap in plastic and let rest for at least 30 minutes.

On a lightly-floured work surface, roll the dough into a long snakelike roll about 1-inch in diameter. Cut the roll into 24 pieces. Keep the unused dough covered with a damp towel as you work.

Use a rolling pin to roll out 1 piece of dough until it is 6 inches in diameter. Sprinkle a tablespoon of scallions over the dough, working them into the dough.

Heat the sesame and coconut oils in a sauté pan. Fry each pancake until golden on both sides.

Dried Fruit Chutney

2 tablespoons butter

2 tablespoons orange zest

1/2 cup dried figs, sliced

1/4 cup dried currants

$^1/2$ cup dried apricots, sliced

1 cup fresh-squeezed orange juice

Slowly cook the butter with the zest, then add the dried fruit and cook until it becomes thick, adding orange juice if necessary. Set aside.

Vegetable Pâté

1 beet, chopped

1 large garlic clove, minced

2 medium leeks, white part only, chopped

6 tablespoons butter, plus extra for the pan

$^1/2$ pound white mushrooms, thinly sliced

10 asparagus stalks

1 carrot, peeled and cut julienne

$^1/2$ cup hempnuts

$2^1/2$ teaspoons thyme, chopped

2 teaspoons sage, chopped

1 teaspoon basil, chopped

3 eggs

1 cup heavy cream

$1^1/2$ tablespoons fresh-squeezed lemon juice

$^1/4$ cup fine bread crumbs

salt and pepper to taste

Preheat the oven to 450°F. Place beet on baking sheet and roast for 30 minutes, or until soft. Peel and chop the beet and set it aside. In a small skillet, sauté the garlic and leeks in the butter until soft. Place the mushrooms, asparagus, carrot, beet, hempnut, thyme, sage, basil, eggs, heavy cream, and lemon juice in a food processor and blend until smooth. Add the sautéed leek and garlic mixture, then mix in the bread crumbs. Add salt and pepper to taste. Lower the oven temperature to 350°F.

Pour the mixture into a loaf pan. Place the loaf pan in a larger pan containing 2 inches of hot water. Cover both pans with aluminum foil and bake for 50 minutes until the pâté is firm to the touch. Allow to cool, then refrigerate overnight before serving to allow the pâté to set.

→

Green Chili Jelly

4 poblano chilies

6–8 tomatillos, husked

1/2 tablespoon scraped fresh ginger root, chopped

1/4 cup fresh coriander, trimmed and lightly packed

1/2 teaspoon salt

1 tablespoon ghee (see Glossary) or vegetable oil

1/2 teaspoon cumin seeds

1/4 teaspoon yellow asafetida powder (see Glossary)

1 envelope gelatin

1/2 cup cold water

1/4 teaspoon freshly ground black pepper

1 teaspoon fresh-squeezed lime juice

Prepare poblano chilies by scorching the skins directly over an open flame or in a broiler. Turn them frequently until blackened on the skins.

Place them in a bowl and seal it with plastic wrap. Allow them to steam and cool down, then peel off their skins, discarding the seeds and stem. Chop them coarsely.

Put the tomatillos, ginger, coriander, and salt in a food processor. Pulse the machine on and off until the ingredients are finely chopped. Heat the ghee or vegetable oil in a saucepan over medium-low heat. When it is hot but not smoking, add the cumin seeds and fry until they darken a few shades. Sprinkle in the asafetida and stir in the chili and the tomatillo mixture within a few seconds.

Cook until pulpy (about 10 minutes).

Dissolve the gelatin in the cold water. Add the dissolved gelatin and mix into the tomatillo pulp. Transfer entire mixture to a serving container and sprinkle with pepper and lime juice. Allow to cool, then refrigerate.

To serve, cut two thin slices of Vegetable Pâté from the loaf and arrange in the center of a plate. Position the Green Chili Jelly, Dried Fruit Chutney, and Hempnut Scallion Pancakes around the pâté.

Hemp Tofu Corndogs

with Celery Root Salad & Pumpkin Seed Oil Dipping Sauce

SERVES 6

Hemp Tofu Corndogs

3/4 cup unbleached white flour
1/4 cup hemp flour
1 cup cornmeal
1 tablespoon sugar
1 tablespoon baking powder
1 teaspoon salt
1 teaspoon chili powder
2 eggs
1 cup Hemp Milk (page 4)
1/4 cup hempseed oil
4 cups coconut oil
1-pound package tofu hotdogs
popsicle sticks

Combine white and hemp flours, cornmeal, sugar, baking powder, salt, and chili powder in a mixing bowl.

Beat the eggs and Hemp Milk with 1/4 cup hempseed oil in a smaller bowl. Pour the liquid ingredients into the dry ingredients and whisk together until batter is smooth.

Heat the coconut oil in a deep heavy pot to 360°F.

Insert a popsicle stick into each hotdog. Using the stick as a handle, dip each hotdog into the batter and turn to coat evenly. Fry the corndogs until golden brown (about 3 to 5 minutes). Remove to paper towels to absorb excess oil.

→

Celery Root Salad

        1 medium celery root
        1 medium cucumber
        1 medium red pepper
        $^1/_2$ pound snow peas

Cut all of the vegetables julienne style and set aside.

Pumpkin Seed Oil Dipping Sauce

        1 teaspoon Dijon mustard
        $^1/_2$ cup apple cider vinegar
        1 cup pumpkin seed oil
        1 teaspoon light brown sugar
        salt and pepper to taste

Combine the Dijon mustard and vinegar in a bowl. Slowly whisk in the pumpkin seed oil until emulsified. Add the sugar and salt and pepper to taste. Set aside.

To serve, mix the Celery Root Salad with a little sauce and place in the middle of a serving plate. Crisscross the Hemp Tofu Corndogs over the salad and serve with the Pumpkin Seed Oil Dipping Sauce.

Hemp was an essential crop to the Mormons when they migrated by covered wagons to the territory now known as Utah.

Hempnut Hummus

SERVES 6

             3 medium eggplants
             5 teaspoons salt
                black pepper and cayenne to taste
                olive oil for brushing
        $1/2$ cup hempnuts
             5 cups chickpeas
          12 garlic cloves
      $1^1/2$ cups tahini (see Glossary)
             1 cup *plus* 4 tablespoons fresh-squeezed lemon juice
             4 teaspoons tamari (see Glossary)
        $1/4$ cup hempseed oil
        $1/4$ cup olive oil
             1 teaspoon paprika
                salt and pepper to taste
        $1/2$ cucumber, sliced
             2 tomatoes, sliced
                Greek or Turkish olives
             1 recipe Hempnut Pita (page 231)

Preheat the oven to 400°F.

Cut the eggplants in half lengthwise and make crisscross incisions all along the insides. Generously sprinkle them with salt and pepper and rub with olive oil. Bake in the oven, uncovered, for 20 to 30 minutes, or until soft and almost mushy. Allow to cool, then scrape the meat from the skins with a spoon.

Place the hempnuts, chickpeas, garlic, tahini, lemon juice, and tamari in a food processor or blender and blend until smooth. Gradually add the hempseed and olive oils. Add the paprika and salt and pepper to taste. Finish by adding the eggplant meat, mixing it in well with a spatula.

Spoon a mound of the hummus on a plate. Make a small well in the center and fill it with hempseed oil. Sprinkle some hempnuts and paprika on top. Surround the mound with sliced cucumbers, tomatoes, and olives. Serve with Hempnut Pita.

Hemp Sweet Potato-Quinoa Soufflé

with Sautéed Spinach & Fried Leeks & Fontina-Celery Root Sauce

SERVES 6

Hemp Sweet Potato-Quinoa Soufflé

4 large sweet potatoes

$1/2$ cup butter

3 eggs, separated

1 cup quinoa, cooked

1 tablespoon garlic, minced

1 teaspoon ground nutmeg

1 teaspoon sage, chopped

1 tablespoon salt

1 tablespoon pepper

extra butter for tins

1 cup fine bread crumbs for tins

Preheat oven to 400°F.

Bake the sweet potatoes for 45 minutes, or until soft. Peel and mash.

Reset oven to 350°F. Add the butter, egg yolks, cooked quinoa, garlic, and spices.

Whisk the egg whites to stiff peaks, then fold into the mixture.

Butter six $3^{1/2}$- x 3-inch baking tins and line them with bread crumbs.

Fill the tins with the mixture to $1/2$ full. Bake in a double boiler covered with aluminum foil for between 30–45 minutes, or until firm. Allow to cool.

Sautéed Spinach & Fried Leeks

2 tablespoons peanut oil

2 teaspoons garlic, minced

2 pounds baby spinach leaves

2 tablespoons soy sauce

pepper to taste

2 cups coconut oil or other high-temperature frying oil

2 leeks, white part only, thinly sliced

1 cup unbleached white flour

Heat the peanut oil in a sauté pan and fry the garlic until golden brown. Add the spinach and cook until wilted. Season with the soy sauce and pepper.

Heat the coconut oil to 350°F. Dust the leeks with flour until coated. Place the leeks into the oil and fry until golden brown. Transfer the leeks to paper towels to absorb the excess oil. Set aside.

Fontina-Celery Root Sauce

$1/2$ cup onions, sliced

$1^1/2$ teaspoons garlic, chopped

$1^1/2$ tablespoons unsalted butter

$1^1/3$ cups celery root, peeled, quartered, and sliced

$1/2$ cup Yukon gold potato, peeled, quartered, and sliced

2–3 cups Vegetable Stock (page 7)

3 cups heavy cream

1 cup fontina cheese, lightly packed and shredded

salt and pepper to taste

$1/2$ cup beurre monte (see Glossary)

1 teaspoon hempseed oil

Cook the onions and garlic in the butter until they are soft and translucent. Add the celery root, potato, and enough Vegetable Stock to cover them. Simmer until the vegetables are tender, then drain. Reserve the liquid.

Puree the vegetables. Add the hempseed oil and beurre monte, and blend until smooth. Pour into a medium saucepan. Add the heavy cream and simmer for about 10 minutes. Whisk in the cheese until it is melted. If the sauce is too thick add some of the reserved stock. Season with salt and pepper to taste.

Serve on a large serving plate with the spinach arranged in the center. Place one Hemp Sweet Potato-Quinoa Soufflé on top of the spinach. Pour the Fontina-Celery Root Sauce over the soufflé and top with fried leeks.

Hempnut Yucca Fritters
with Mushroom & Herb Stuffing

SERVES 6

Mushroom & Herb Stuffing

4 tablespoons butter

2 garlic cloves, minced

1 small onion, minced

1 tablespoon dry sherry

1/2 pound button mushrooms, cut into small pieces

1/4 pound oyster mushrooms, cut into small pieces

1/4 pound shiitake mushrooms, cut into small pieces

salt and pepper to taste

2 tablespoons fresh thyme, chopped

Warm the butter in a skillet and sauté the garlic and onion until translucent. Add the dry sherry and the button, oyster, and shiitake mushrooms and sauté until soft. Season with salt and pepper to taste. Add thyme and allow to cool to room temperature.

Hempnut Yucca Fritters

14 cups cold water

salt

2 1/2 pounds yucca, cut crosswise into 2-inch pieces and peeled

1 cup unbleached white flour

ground black pepper

6 egg whites, lightly beaten

1/2 cup dry bread crumbs, lightly toasted

1/2 cup hempnuts

Pour 12 cups water into a large pot. Lightly salt the water and bring to a boil over high heat. Add the yucca to the pot and cook for 10 minutes. Add 1 cup of cold water and cook for an additional 5 minutes. Repeat again with the remaining cup of water (adding cold water helps tenderize the yucca). Drain and let cool completely. Remove any remaining fibers. Place the yucca in a bowl and mash it into a smooth paste. If too dry, add some water. Let cool to room temperature and refrigerate for at least 6 hours and up to 24 hours.

Divide the yucca into 12 even pieces and roll each piece into a ball. Make a depression in the center of each ball with your thumb. Put 1 tablespoon of the stuffing into each ball. Pinch the top of each ball closed with your fingers. Gently roll the balls into an oval shape between the palms of your hands.

Preheat the oven to 400°F. Coat a non-stick baking sheet with non-stick vegetable spray.

Set out 3 bowls. Place the flour and pepper in the first, the egg whites in the second, and the bread crumbs and hempnuts in the third. Dip each fritter in the flour, then in the egg whites, and finally in the bread crumb-hempnuts mixture. Shake off the excess bread crumbs. Arrange the fritters on a baking tray and spray the tops with a little non-stick spray. Bake for 20 minutes or until crisp and golden brown. Serve.

 Hemp requires little water and can be grown in all 50 of the United States.

Vegetable Hempura

SERVES 4

Vegetables

    1 medium sweet potato, sliced into thin disks
    8 asparagus stalks, sliced in half
    2 medium Japanese eggplants, thinly sliced
    2 carrots, sliced into thin disks
    1 package enoki mushrooms, stems discarded

Hempura Batter

    $1/2$ cup hempnuts
    $3/8$ cup unbleached white flour
    $1/8$ cup hemp flour
    1 egg white
    1 cup club soda
    4 cups coconut oil or other high-temperature frying oil

Whisk together hempnuts, white and hemp flours, egg white, and club soda. Do not overmix. Dip vegetables in Hempura Batter and fry at 350°F until golden and crispy.

Ponzu Dipping Sauce

    $1/4$ cup mirin (see Glossary)
    $1/4$ cup soy sauce
    1 tablespoon ginger
    $1/8$ cup fresh-squeezed lemon juice
    1 tablespoon sugar
    strained liquid from rehydrated hijiki (see Glossary)

Whisk together all ingredients and set aside.

Garnish: 1 tablespoon black sesame seeds
    $1/2$ bunch scallions, thinly sliced

To serve, arrange Vegetable Hempura on a serving plate with Ponzu Dipping Sauce. Garnish with black sesame seeds and scallions.

Poblano Chilies Stuffed with Corn

SERVES 6

    3 ears corn
    8 poblano chili peppers
    1/2 cup sharp white cheddar cheese, grated
    3 scallions, trimmed and minced
    1 garlic clove, minced
    1/4 cup fresh cilantro, chopped
    3 tablespoons currants
    salt and pepper to taste
    1 cup unbleached white flour
    8 egg whites, lightly beaten
    3/4 cup unseasoned dry bread crumbs
    1/4 cup stone-ground blue cornmeal
    1/2 cup hempnuts, toasted
    bed of lettuce
    Southwestern Aioli (page 78)

Coat the ears of corn with oil and place on a grill, turning occasionally for 2 to 3 minutes on each side, until the whole corn is well browned on all sides. Allow to cool and cut the kernels off the corn cobs. Set aside in a bowl.

Meanwhile, roast the poblano chilies over an open flame until charred. Transfer to a bowl, cover with plastic wrap, and allow to steam until cool. Once cooled, scrape off and discard the skins.

Set 6 of the chilies aside. Core, seed, and cut the flesh of the remaining 2 chilies into 1/4-inch pieces. Add to the corn kernels. Stir in the cheese, scallions, garlic, fresh cilantro, and currants. Season with salt and pepper to taste.

Carefully make a 2-inch long incision along one side of each of the remaining 6 chilies. Use a spoon to scrape out the seeds and the core, leaving the stem intact. Stuff each pepper with the corn mixture.

Preheat oven to 400°F.

Set out 3 bowls. Place the flour in the first, the egg whites in the second, and mix the bread crumbs, hempnuts, and cornmeal in the third. (Mix these last ingredients with your fingertips.) Dip each chili: first in the flour, shaking off the excess, then in the egg, then in the crumb mixture. Place the chilies on a non-stick baking sheet. Bake for 20 minutes, or until golden brown and the filling is hot. Serve over the bed of lettuce and drizzle with Southwestern Aioli.

Hemp Deviled Eggs

MAKES 12 OPEN-FACED EGG HALVES

6 eggs, hard boiled
3 tablespoons mayonnaise
1 teaspoon Dijon mustard
1 tablespoon hempseed oil
1 teaspoon paprika
1 teaspoon salt
1/2 teaspoon ground white pepper
1 teaspoon chives, finely chopped

Cut the eggs in half and remove the yolks from the whites, being careful not to break the egg whites. Place the yolks in a stainless steel bowl.

Mash the yolks with a fork. Add the mayonnaise, Dijon mustard, hempseed oil, and spices. Mix until smooth.

Transfer mixture into a pastry bag and fill the halved egg whites. Top with a sprinkle of chopped chives. Arrange on a serving tray.

Stuffed Artichokes

with Hempnut Romesco Sauce

SERVES 4

Artichokes

>8 artichokes (size of preference)
>
>2 ears corn
>
>>hempseed oil for brushing
>
>1 roasted red pepper, diced
>
>1 asparagus stalk, diced
>
>3 fennel, diced

Start cleaning the artichokes by pulling back the leaves. Once the choke (the inside of the flower) is exposed, trim the dark green skin of the artichoke. Place artichokes in a large pot of salted boiling water and cook until tender (at least 15 minutes). Remove the artichokes to an ice bath. Remove the choke with a spoon. Slice 4 artichokes lengthwise to form 8 halves. Leave the remaining 4 artichokes in the form of a natural cup.

Remove the corn from its husks and brush with hempseed oil. Roast the ears in the oven or on the grill. Remove the corn from the cob with a knife. Place the fennel and asparagus in separate pots of salted boiling water until they are tender. Dice fennel, asparagus, and roasted red peppers into 1-inch square pieces. Combine the corn kernels and diced vegetables and stuff the 4 artichoke cups. Set side.

→

Hempnut Romesco Sauce

    2 roasted red peppers
    4 plum tomatoes
    1 teaspoon white pepper
    1 teaspoon red pepper flakes
    1/2 teaspoon cayenne pepper
    2 garlic cloves
    1/4 cup hempnuts, toasted
    2 slices toasted or dried-out bread
    2 tablespoons red wine vinegar
        salt and pepper to taste

Combine all ingredients in a blender and puree until smooth. Season with salt and pepper to taste. Set aside.

Golden Raisin Vinaigrette

    1 teaspoon Dijon mustard
    1/4 cup golden raisins
    3 tablespoons rice wine vinegar
    1/2 cup hempseed oil

Mix the Dijon mustard, golden raisins, and rice wine vinegar in a blender until pureed. Slowly add the hempseed oil until an emulsion forms.

To serve, spread a full ladle of Hempnut Romesco Sauce in the center of a serving plate. Place the eight sliced artichoke halves crisscrossed in the center of the plate. Arrange the 4 Stuffed Artichokes around the halves. Dress the artichokes with the Golden Raisin Vinaigrette. Serve at room temperature.

Hemp Cheese Sticks

YIELDS 8 STICKS

1 cup Hemp Cheese (page 5)
  unbleached white flour for dredging
2 egg whites
1 cup panko bread crumbs (see Glossary)
2 cups coconut oil or other high-temperature frying oil
  salt to taste

Make sure cheese has been pressed for at least 24 hours. Divide the cheese into 8 even portions. Form each one into a rectangular log shape. Dredge first in flour, then egg whites, and last in finely-ground panko bread crumbs. Fry at 375°F for approximately 2 minutes, or until golden brown. Season with salt to taste. Serve with Hemp Marinara (page 81) or your favorite aioli.

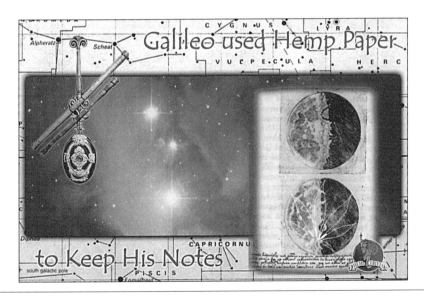

From prior to 1000 B.C. until 1883 A.D., cannabis hemp was our planet's largest agricultural crop, producing the majority of Earth's fiber, fabric, lighting oil, paper, incense, and medicines. In addition, it was a primary source of essential food oil and protein for humans and animals.

Korean Seitan Lettuce Wraps

SERVES 6 TO 8

    2 pounds ground seitan (see Glossary)

    1 red pepper, diced

    $1/2$ cup scallions, sliced

    $1/4$ cup ground peanuts

    $1/4$ cup raisins, chopped

    3 tablespoons sweet sirloin sauce

    2 tablespoons soy sauce

    3 tablespoons fresh-squeezed lime juice

    2 tablespoons fish sauce

    4 tablespoons hempseed oil

    $1/4$ cup hempnuts

    1 head Boston bibb lettuce, rinsed

Garnish: black sesame seeds

    $1/2$ cup fresh water chestnuts, cut julienne

    1 daikon radish, peeled and spun on a mandolin (see Glossary)

Mix together all the ingredients except the lettuce and garnish.

Peel the Boston bibb lettuce leaves from the head and arrange 4 large or 5 small leaves on a serving plate. Fill with the seitan mixture.

Place water chestnuts and daikon over the filling and sprinkle some black sesame seeds around as a garnish. Serve with a ramekin of Banana Sambal (page 64).

Quasars

I've been criticized in the past for nomenclature that begs definition. Here we find a set of recipes that can only be described as "out there," so what better title than Quasar? We've taken a set of vegetarian recipes and given you the "steak," using tofu with a Native American Indian succotash. Travel to Austria and make your own Speckknodel, or go south to Cuba for Garlic Hempnut Tamales with with Corn-Green Pepper Salsa. If you're bored, why not fly over to Spain for some Stuffed Piquillo Peppers, or sail the Caribbean in search of a unique Puerto Rican Mofongo stuffed in a sweet acorn squash. Too risky? Then make Hempizza and stay home and rent a movie. Personally, I dream of Hawaiian days with Mama Mojo's Platanos and surfing The Big One. When I come down to earth, I just settle for a picnic with a Green Bean-Walnut Hemp Burger and watch the clouds roll on by. Stay hempy!

Hempnut Johnny Cakes

with Spicy Vegetable Ragout & Tamarind Agave Nectar

SERVES 6

Hempnut Johnny Cakes

      2 cups cornmeal
      1 cup unbleached white flour
      1 cup hempnuts
   1/4 cup sugar
      2 teaspoons salt
      2 eggs, beaten
 1 1/2 cups water

Preheat oven to 500°F.

Combine the cornmeal, flour, hempnuts, sugar, and salt in a stainless steel bowl and mix well. Make a well in the center of the mixture and add beaten eggs and water. Whisk ingredients together until combined.

Oil two cookie sheets and heap tablespoon-size balls of batter to form eighteen 3-inch cakes. Cook the cakes in the oven for 3 to 4 minutes, or until bottoms are lightly brown and tops have set. Turn over once and cook another 2 to 3 minutes.

Spicy Vegetable Ragout

        vegetable oil
1^1/2 cups white onions, diced
1^1/2 cups yellow squash, 1-inch diced
1^1/2 cups red peppers, 1-inch diced
1^1/2 cups plum tomatoes, 1-inch diced
    3 jalapeño peppers, seeded and chopped
    1 tablespoon fresh thyme
      salt and pepper to taste

Heat vegetable oil in a saucepan. Add the vegetables and sauté until all the vegetables are browning on the edges. Add thyme and salt and pepper to taste. Cook over medium heat for 5 to 10 minutes. Set aside.

Tamarind Agave Nectar

    ^{1}/4 cup tamarind syrup (see Glossary)
    ^{1}/2 cup agave nectar (see Glossary) or honey

To serve, mound a cup of vegetable ragout on a plate. Surround with three Johnny Cakes. Make the Tamarind Agave Nectar drizzle by whisking agave nectar and tamarind syrup, then lightly coat the cakes. Top the vegetable ragout with a sprig of thyme and sprinkle with hempnuts. Serve.

In the 1950s in Southern Africa, mothers of the Sotho tribe served ground hempseed "with bread or mealie pap" to children during weaning.
—Kenneth Jones, *Nutritional and Medicinal Guide to Hemp Seed*, 1995

Green Bean-Walnut Hemp Burgers

Serves 6

1 pound fresh green beans
3/8 cup extra virgin olive oil
1 large Spanish onion, diced
4 garlic cloves, diced
salt and pepper to taste
1/2 cup walnuts
1/8 cup hempseed oil
1/2 cup panko bread crumbs (see Glossary)
2 eggs, beaten (optional)
1 tablespoon vegetable oil
6 Hemp Rolls (page 229)

Cook the green beans in salted boiling water until tender (about 6 minutes). Remove to an ice bath.

Add 1 tablespoon of olive oil to a sauté pan. Over low heat, cook the onions and garlic, until onions are soft and translucent. Make sure they don't brown. Season with salt and pepper to taste and allow to cool.

Place cooked green beans in a food processor and spin until beans have the consistency of creamed corn. Remove to a metal bowl.

Place the walnuts in the food processor and pulse 6 times. Walnut pieces should be the size of peppercorns or smaller. Add to the same metal bowl. Mix in the onion and garlic mixture. Add the remaining olive and hempseed oils. Stir together well.

Fold the panko bread crumbs and eggs (optional) into mixture and form into burger patties. The entire 1/2 cup of bread crumbs may or may not be needed. The consistency should be a little looser than a regular beef hamburger.

Add vegetable oil to a sauté pan over medium heat. Place burgers in pan and cook through on both sides. If egg is not used to bind burgers, be careful when you flip the burgers or they will fall apart.

Serve in a Hemp Roll with onions, tomatoes, lettuce, pickles, and your sauce of choice.

Hempnut Lentil Stew with Speckknodel

SERVES 6

2 medium onions, chopped
1 parsnip, sliced
2 medium carrots, sliced
4 tablespoons hempseed oil
1 pound dried lentils, washed and drained
1 cup celery, sliced
5 cups water
salt and pepper to taste
2 whole cloves
2 bay leaves
1 large potato
1/4 cup Hempnut Butter (page 4)
1/4 cup (1/2 stick) butter
2 tablespoons apple cider vinegar
1 recipe Hemp Speckknodel (page 131)

Sweat the onions, parsnip, and carrots in 2 tablespoons hempseed oil until the onions are golden.

Add the lentils, celery, water, and seasonings. Grate the raw potato into the mixture.

Simmer covered for 1 hour, until lentils and vegetables are tender. Remove bay leaves and add the Hempnut Butter and regular butter. Add vinegar just before serving.

Serve hot in a bowl with Hemp Speckknodel. Drizzle with remaining hempseed oil.

Hemp Speckknodel

SERVES 6

> 1 white onion, chopped
> 2 tablespoons butter
> 5 dry bread rolls, chopped
> 2 tablespoons Hemp Milk (page 4)
> 2 eggs
> salt to taste
> 1 teaspoon parsley, chopped
> 1/4 cup prosciutto, chopped
> 2 tablespoons hempseed oil
> 2 tablespoons hempnuts
> 1/4 cup unbleached white flour

Sweat the onion in the butter in a sauté pan. Remove to a bowl. Add the dry bread and mix. In a separate stainless steel bowl, beat the Hemp Milk, eggs, salt, and parsley together. Mix into the onion-bread mixture. Allow to sit for 20 minutes. Add the prosciutto, hempseed oil, and hempnuts, and mix well. Work the flour into the mixture by adding lukewarm water, teaspoon by teaspoon, until the dough is rolled into 6 firm knodel balls. Boil the knodels in a pot of boiling salted water. Lower the heat and simmer for about 20 minutes. Drain.

Serve with Hempnut Lentil Stew, or as an accompaniment to a salad, meat dish, or broth soup.

Hemp is the strongest, most durable, longest lasting natural soft fiber on the planet.

BBQ Seitan

with Grilled Corn & Spinach over Garlic Rice

SERVES 4

BBQ Sauce

3 tablespoons vegetable oil

1 medium vidalia onion (see Glossary), chopped

4 garlic cloves, chopped

1 cup light brown sugar, packed

1 cup sherry vinegar

1 teaspoon cayenne pepper

2 teaspoons Tabasco sauce

2 cups ketchup

1/4 cup Dijon mustard

1 tablespoon Worcestershire sauce

Heat 1 tablespoon of vegetable oil in a sauté pan over medium heat. Cook chopped onion and garlic until translucent. Use a wooden spoon to mix in brown sugar until it dissolves and begins to bubble. Add the sherry vinegar and allow it to reduce for about 5 minutes. Add cayenne pepper, Tabasco sauce, and ketchup and bring to a simmer. Stir occasionally. Pull pan off the burner and stir in the Dijon mustard and Worcestershire sauce.

Seitan, Spinach, and Corn

4 ears corn

1 tablespoon butter

salt and pepper to taste

1 tablespoon vegetable oil

2 pounds spinach

1 pound seitan (see Glossary), cut into chunks

1/3 cup hempnuts, toasted

Remove the corn from its husks and cut into rounds. Melt the butter in a pan over medium heat and add corn. Cook for about 3 minutes per side. Season with salt and pepper to taste.

→

Add the vegetable oil to the pan and turn to high heat. Cook the spinach until it begins to wilt.

Place the seitan in a large skillet. Cover the seitan with BBQ Sauce. Cook thoroughly. Mix in the toasted hempnuts.

Garlic Rice

$1^1/2$ cups jasmine rice, or other long-grain white rice
1 tablespoon olive oil
1 shallot, chopped
4 garlic cloves, chopped
$2^3/4$ cups water
salt and pepper to taste

Rinse the rice with water. Heat the olive oil in a saucepan over medium heat. Add the shallot and garlic. Cook for 3 minutes. Add the rice and water and bring to a boil. Turn the heat down and cover. Cook the rice at a simmer for about 17 minutes. Remove from the heat when the water is completely absorbed. Season with salt and pepper to taste.

To serve, place the Garlic Rice in the center of a bowl, followed by the spinach and BBQ Seitan. Place corn rounds around the bowl.

Mama Mojo's Platanos
with Chili Sambal, Jalapeño Salsa, & Coconut Sambal

SERVES 6

Chili Sambal

> 1^1/$_2$ lime skins
> 2 garlic cloves
> 2-inch piece ginger
> ^{1}/$_4$ cup brown sugar
> 2 teaspoons salt
> 1^1/$_2$ medium white onions
> 4 teaspoons crushed red pepper
> ^{1}/$_2$ cup hempnuts
> ^{1}/$_4$ teaspoon white distilled vinegar
> 1 cup peanut oil

Chop the lime skins. Place in a food processor and mince as finely as possible. Add the garlic, ginger, sugar, and salt to the processor and continue to chop. Add the onions and partially chop. Add the crushed red pepper, hempnuts, and vinegar and blend entire mixture to an even consistency. Fry the mix in the peanut oil, stirring constantly until the color changes and the oil bleeds out.

Jalapeño Salsa

> 6 plum tomatoes, diced
> 1 small red onion, diced
> ^{1}/$_2$ bunch cilantro, chopped
> juice of 1 lime
> 1 tablespoon olive oil
> 1 jalapeño, deseeded and chopped
> salt and pepper to taste

Mix all the ingredients and refrigerate.

→

Coconut Sambal

        4 garlic cloves
    1/4 cup crushed red pepper
    1/4 cup brown sugar
    1/4 cup cumin
        1 cup distilled white vinegar
       12 ounces dried unsweetened coconut
        4 lime skins

Place the garlic, crushed red pepper, sugar, and cumin in a food processor. Blend thoroughly. Add the vinegar and continue to blend. Remove the mixture and place in a medium-sized bowl. Clean and dry the food processor. Add the dried coconut to the food processor and finely chop. Heat a large sauce pan and combine the mixture with the chopped coconut. Add the lime skins Cook until the color turns and the sauce is reduced. It is finished when it is dry and pasty.

Mama Mojo's Platanos

        2 tablespoons granulated sugar
        2 tablespoons cinnamon, ground
        1 teaspoon nutmeg, ground
        1 ripe yellow plantain
        1 tablespoon butter
    1/2 bunch scallions, chopped
        1 teaspoon chili sambal
        1 ounce mesclun greens
        1 teaspoon olive oil
        1 wedge of lime
          Hemp Maize Bread (page 237)
          Chocolate Banana Bread (page 241)
        2 tablespoons Jalapeño Salsa
        1 teaspoon Coconut Sambal
        1 teaspoon Mexican chocolate, shaved

Mix the sugar, cinnamon, and nutmeg in a bowl. Peel the plantain and cut on a bias to a 1/4-inch thickness. Place the plantain pieces in the sugar mixture. Heat a sauté pan and add the butter, scallions, and Chili Sambal. Cook on medium heat, stirring often so that the scallions don't burn. Add the sugar-coated plantains to the sauté pan. Flip them over until they are golden brown and tender to the touch.

To serve, place the mesclun greens at the top of the serving plate. Drizzle the olive oil and lime juice over the greens. Place the cooked plantains criss-cross down the center of the plate. Cut the Maize and Chocolate Banana Breads 1-inch thick and arrange beside the plantains. Spoon the Jalapeño Salsa directly onto the place where the breads meet the plate. Sprinkle the Coconut Sambal and the Mexican chocolate all over the top.

In Ancient Egypt the Pharohs used Hemp in Building the Pyramids

The earliest known woven fabric was apparently of hemp, which began to be worked in the eighth millennium (8,000–7,000 B.C.).—*The Columbia History of the World*, 1981, page 54

Spicy Seitan Tamales
with Corn-Green Pepper Salsa

SERVES 4

Tamales

    1 head garlic, cut in half
    1 1/2 tablespoons plus 1 teaspoon olive oil
    3 serrano chilies
    2 eggs
    1 cup whole milk
    2 tablespoons butter
    1/2 cup hempnuts
    1 cup cornmeal
    1 cup unbleached white flour
    4 tablespoons sugar
    1 tablespoon baking powder
    salt to taste
    8 ounces seitan (see Glossary), chopped small
    6 corn husks

Preheat over to 350°F. Place both halves of the garlic head in aluminum foil and drizzle 1 teaspoon olive oil over it. Wrap and bake for 30 minutes, or until tender and lightly brown. Remove the garlic from its skin and mash with a fork. Add together along with the remaining olive oil, serrano chilies, eggs, milk, and butter.

Combine the hempnuts, cornmeal, white flour, sugar, baking powder, and a pinch of salt in a mixing bowl. Add wet ingredients to dry ingredients and stir with wooden spoon until smooth. Refrigerate for about 1 hour. Mix in seitan.

Carefully fill cornhusks with tamale mixture and wrap. Place a bamboo steamer over boiling water and gently place the tamales inside. Steam for 7 minutes.

Corn-Green Pepper Salsa

      2 scallions, thinly sliced

      1 ear corn

      1 green pepper, diced

      2 plum tomatoes, diced

      2 garlic cloves, diced

      1 bunch cilantro

       salt and pepper to taste

Combine scallions, corn, green pepper, tomatoes, garlic, and cilantro leaves. Season with salt and pepper to taste. Allow salsa to sit at room temperature for at least 20 minutes.

To serve, open the cornhusks to expose the tamales. Spoon the Corn-Green Pepper Salsa over the Spicy Seitan Tamales.

 Hemp clothing typically lasts ten years, compared to five for cotton.

Stuffed Spanish Piquillo Peppers
with Lemon Hemp Vinaigrette

SERVES 4

Stuffed Peppers

> 1 cup couscous (see Glossary)
> 1 tablespoon butter
> 1/3 cup boiling water
> salt and pepper to taste
> 1 bunch asparagus, diced
> 1/2 bulb fennel, diced
> 1 teaspoon lemon zest
> 1/4 cup hempnuts, toasted
> 3 plum tomatoes, diced
> 1/2 cup prunes, diced
> 1 20-ounce can piquillo peppers (see Glossary)

Preheat oven to 300°F. In a bowl, add couscous and butter to boiling water. Stir together, season with salt and pepper, and cover with plastic wrap. Let stand at room temperature for 20 to 25 minutes. Fluff the couscous with a fork to separate grains once the water is completely absorbed.

Separately blanche the asparagus and fennel. Remove to an ice bath.

Zest a lemon with a zester or grater. Place the lemon zest, fennel, asparagus, hempnuts, tomatoes, and prunes in a bowl. Add the couscous and mix all the ingredients together.

Drain the can of piquillo peppers. Use a teaspoon to stuff the peppers with the couscous mixture. Set the peppers aside.

→

Vegetables

    2 tablespoons peanut oil

    2 garlic cloves, minced

    4 medium baby bok choy (see Glossary)

    8 ounces baby spinach

      salt and pepper to taste

Heat the peanut oil in a sauté pan. Fry the garlic until golden brown and the bok choy until tender. Add the spinach and cook until wilted. Season with salt and pepper to taste.

Lemon Hemp Vinaigrette

    1 garlic clove, minced

    1 shallot, minced

      juice of 1 lemon

    4 tablespoons hempseed oil

      salt and pepper to taste

Combine the minced garlic and shallot. Add lemon juice and let stand at room temperature for 10 minutes. Whisk in the hempseed oil. Season with salt and pepper to taste.

To prepare, drizzle some Lemon Hemp Vinaigrette over the Stuffed Spanish Piquillo Peppers and place in the preheated oven for 4 to 5 minutes. Cut in half lengthwise to form open halves. On a serving plate, wrap the baby bok choy leaves around the spinach. Drizzle the remaining vinaigrette over the greens. Place a pepper in the center of each bok choy cup. Serve.

Caribbean Mofongo
with Spinach & Soy Hemp Sauce

SERVES 6

Mofongo

6 plantains
4 tablespoons olive oil
3 garlic cloves, chopped
18 ounces seitan (see Glossary), cut into chunks
1 medium yucca
3 poblano chilies, roasted, seeded, and chopped
3 very ripe bananas
1/2 bunch cilantro, chopped
2 tablespoons agave nectar (see Glossary), honey, or light corn syrup
1 tablespoon chili-garlic sauce (see Glossary)
salt and pepper to taste
coconut oil or other high-temperature frying oil
1/2 bunch scallions, thinly sliced
3 medium acorn squashes
agave nectar to brush acorn squash
butter to brush acorn squash

Peel, cut, and soak the plantains in salted water for 20 minutes. Drain well. Heat the olive oil in a sauté pan. Fry the plantains on high heat, until soft and golden (about 5 minutes). Remove to paper towels to absorb excess oil.

Reheat the olive oil and lightly brown the garlic. Add the seitan and fry until crispy, but not dry. Peel the yucca and boil it until soft. Roast the poblano chilies over an open flame. Deseed and chop. Mix together the ripe bananas, yucca, and chilies. Mash the ingredients together, adding the cilantro, agave nectar, and chili-garlic sauce. Season with salt and pepper to taste and set aside.

Preheat oven to 400°F.

Split the squashes in half lengthwise and deseed. Season with agave nectar, butter, and salt and pepper to taste. Roast in the oven for approximately 1 hour, or until tender.

→

Spinach

        2 tablespoons peanut oil

        3 garlic cloves, minced

        2 small carrots, cut julienne

1 1/2 pounds baby spinach

        soy sauce

Heat the oil in a sauté pan. Add the garlic and carrots. Cook for 1 minute. Add the spinach and sauté for 2 minutes. Finish with a splash of soy sauce.

Soy Hemp Sauce

        2 cups soy sauce

1/4 cup honey

3/8 cup hempnuts

        1 tablespoon red peppers, minced

        3 tablespoons tomatoes, chopped

Add all ingredients to a pot.

    Reduce the mixture to one-third, mixing occasionally, over medium heat. Set aside.

To prepare, reheat the mofongo in a sauté pan and, if necessary, reconstitute with water. Place the mofongo in the acorn squash halves and season with Soy Hemp Sauce.

Garnish:

1/4 cup hempnuts

1/2 bunch scallions, thinly sliced

To serve, place the sautéed spinach in the center of a serving plate. Put the stuffed acorn squash on top of the spinach. Sprinkle with hempnuts and scallions.

Vegetable Hempizza

with Huacatay Pesto

Serves 6

Hempizza Dough

1 pound unbleached white flour

$1/2$ pound hemp flour

$1/4$ cup sterilized hempseed

$1/4$ cup hempnuts

1 package active dry yeast

$4^1/2$ cups warm water *plus* extra if needed

2 tablespoons garlic, minced

$1/2$ cup *plus* 1 tablespoon hempseed oil

1 tablespoon salt

1 teaspoon cayenne pepper

Preheat oven to 450°F.

Put the white and hemp flours, hempseed, and hempnuts in an electric mixer fitted with a dough hook. Combine the yeast and $1/2$ cup warm water in a small bowl. Set aside. In a separate bowl, combine the remaining 4 cups of water, garlic, hempseed oil, salt, and cayenne pepper and mix with the mixer on low speed. Turn the mixer on medium and add the yeast mixture. Mix until it is smooth and not sticking to the side. (If it is sticking, add a handful of flour.)

Remove the dough and form into a ball. Place it in a bowl and pour the tablespoon of hempseed oil over it. Work the oil so it covers the dough. Seal the bowl with plastic wrap. Let sit for 30 minutes. Remove the dough and work it into a long sausage shape. Cut into 6 equal pieces. Knead each piece into a ball, wrap with plastic wrap, and let sit covered for 15 minutes on a cookie sheet. Use a rolling pin to roll each ball into a 10-inch circle. Put each one in an 8-inch deep-dish pizza pan and roll the edges in to make a crust. Bake the pizza crusts until slightly golden (about 10 minutes). Set aside.

→

Huacatay Pesto

    1 4-ounce package frozen huacatay (see Glossary), minced
    1 4-ounce package frozen albahaca (see Glossary), minced
    1 tablespoon garlic, minced
  1/4 cup hempnuts
  1/4 cup parmesan, grated
    2 tablespoons hempseed oil
    2 tablespoons olive oil
    1 teaspoon salt
    1 teaspoon pepper

Place all ingredients in a blender or food processor and blend until smooth.

Toppings

    2 thin green zucchini, thinly sliced on a bias
    2 thin yellow zucchini or crooked neck squash, thinly sliced on a bias
  1/2 cup olive oil
    1 cup sun-dried tomatoes
    2 8-ounce packages feta cheese
     salt and pepper to taste

Preheat oven to 500°F. Mix the sliced zucchini and yellow squash together in a bowl with the olive oil and add salt and pepper to taste. Place the slices on a non-stick baking tray and roast uncovered in the oven for 20 minutes, or until golden brown. Soak the sun-dried tomatoes in warm water for 10 minutes. Slice into pieces and set aside.

Prepare the Vegetable Hempizzas by spreading 2 tablespoons of Huacatay Pesto on each crust. Arrange the zucchini and squash on top of the pesto. Sprinkle with sun-dried tomatoes and crumbled feta cheese. Bake in the oven for 10 minutes at 450°F, until cheese is melted and crust is golden. Serve.

Hempnut-Crusted Stuffed Hearts of Palm

with Pinto Bean Medley

SERVES 6

Pinto Bean Medley

> 1 tablespoon butter
> 3 garlic cloves, minced
> 1 small white onion, diced
> 2 celery stalks, diced
> 1 leek, diced
> 1 large carrot, diced
> 2 20-ounce cans hearts of palm in water
> 2 20-ounce cans pinto beans
> 2 plum tomatoes, deseeded and diced
> 1 cup Vegetable Stock (page 7)
> salt and pepper to taste

Heat the butter in a pan. Sauté the garlic and onion until translucent. Add the celery, leek, and carrot and sauté for 2 minutes.

Remove and dice the center of the heart of palm, and set the rest aside.

Add the beans, tomatoes, and diced hearts of palm to the pan. Add the Vegetable Stock and allow to reduce by half at a low simmer. Make sure that all the vegetables are tender but not overcooked. Add salt and pepper to taste and set aside.

Stuffing

  1 cup Pinto Bean Medley

  1 4-ounce container Mascarpone cheese

  3 tablespoons bread crumbs

  1 tablespoon hempseed oil

  salt and pepper to taste

Put 1 cup of the bean mixture in a food processor, add the Mascarpone cheese, bread crumbs, hempseed oil, and salt and pepper to taste. Blend until smooth.

Stuffed Hearts of Palm

  1 cup unbleached white flour

  1 cup whole milk

  1 cup hempnuts

  peanut oil for frying

  $1/4$ cup parsley, minced

Use a spoon to fill the hearts of palm with the stuffing.

Place the flour, milk, and hempnuts in three separate bowls. Dredge the stuffed hearts of palm in the flour, shaking off any excess, then in the milk, and finally in the hempnuts, making sure that all sides are covered.

Heat some peanut oil in a pan and fry the hearts of palm until golden on all sides.

To serve, heat the Pinto Bean Medley and place in the middle of a serving plate. Cut the Hempnut-Crusted Stuffed Hearts of Palm in half and arrange on top of the beans. Drizzle with a little hempseed oil. Sprinkle with minced parsley.

During its first 150 years, *The Encyclopedia Britannica* was printed primarily on paper produced with hemp.

Seitan Vegetable Hemp Tortilla Enchiladas

with Jalapeño-Turmeric Rice

SERVES 6

Hemp Tortillas

    1¹/4 cups masa harina (see Glossary)
    ¹/4 cup hemp flour
    2 teaspoons salt
    2 teaspoons vegetable shortening
    1¹/4 cups water

Stir together the masa harina, hemp flour, and salt in a mixing bowl.

Melt the shortening together with the water in a small pot over high heat, until boiling and melted. Pour this mixture into the masa harina and mix to form a ball. Knead the dough on a lightly-floured work surface for about 5 minutes, or until smooth. Divide the dough into 6 even pieces and pat each one out between your palms until it is 2 inches in diameter. With a rolling pin, roll out each portion of dough between pieces of parchment paper until it is paper thin and about 12 inches in diameter. Heat a large cast iron or other heavy skillet until just lightly smoking. Remove 1 of the tortillas from the paper and place it in the skillet. Cook for about 30 seconds on each side, or until golden.

Keep warm in a cloth towel. Repeat until all are cooked.

Enchiladas

    12 tablespoons peanut oil
    1¹/2 cups white onion, sliced
    1¹/2 cups red and green peppers, sliced
    12 ounces seitan (see Glossary), cut in small pieces
    3 cups black beans
       salt and pepper to taste
    12 8-inch Hemp Tortillas
    1¹/2 pounds mozzarella, shredded
    2 cups Hemp Mole Sauce (page 80)
       salt and pepper to taste
    6 scallions, sliced for garnish

Heat the oil in a skillet and sauté onion and peppers until soft.

Add seitan and black beans. Season with salt and pepper to taste.

Separate the mixture into the 12 parts and roll them up in the tortillas. Slice the enchiladas in half on a bias and place in a casserole dish. Cover with the mozzarella cheese and place under broiler until melted.

Jalapeño-Turmeric Rice

> 1 tablespoon vegetable oil
> 1 tablespoon jalapeño, chopped
> 1 garlic clove, minced
> 1 1/2 cups white rice
> 1 tablespoon ground turmeric
> salt and pepper
> 3 cups water

Heat the oil in a pot and sauté the jalapeño and garlic and for 1 minute. Add the rice and mix. Add the turmeric and mix thoroughly. Season with salt and pepper.

Add the water and bring to a boil. Cover and reduce to medium-low heat. Simmer for 15–20 minutes, or until the water is evaporated and the rice is cooked.

To serve, place a serving of Jalapeño-Turmeric Rice and 2 Seitan Vegetable Hemp Tortilla Enchiladas on each plate. Ladle Hemp Mole Sauce over the enchiladas and sprinkle with scallions.

Hempnut-Crusted Tofu Steak
with Jalapeño-Agave Succotash

SERVES 6

Tofu Steak

     2 pounds firm tofu packaged in water
     $1^1/2$ cups cornmeal
     $1/2$ cup hempnuts
     4 cups coconut oil or other high-temperature frying oil

Cut the tofu into 6 even, rectangular pieces. Mix the cornmeal and hempnuts together in a bowl. Dredge the tofu in the hempnut-cornmeal mix (making sure to press the tofu well so that the mixture sticks). Heat the coconut oil to 350°F. Drop in the tofu steak in and fry until golden brown (about 2 minutes). Transfer to paper towels to absorb excess oil. Set aside.

Jalapeño-Agave Succotash

     1 tablespoon butter
     2 garlic cloves, minced
     1 medium red onion, diced
     2 cups corn kernels
     1 cup red pepper, diced
     3 tablespoons agave nectar (see Glossary) or honey
     salt and pepper to taste
     $1/2$ cup tomatoes, diced
     $1/2$ cup black beans, cooked or canned
     1 cup scallions, chopped
     1 jalapeño, deseeded and minced
     2 tablespoons fresh-squeezed lime juice
     3 tablespoons kecap manis (see Glossary)

Heat the butter in a sauté pan. Sauté the garlic and red onion until they start to turn golden. Add the corn, red pepper, and agave nectar. Sauté for 2 minutes. Add salt and pepper to taste. Add the tomatoes, black beans, scallions, jalapeño, and lime juice. Sauté for an additional 2 minutes.

→

To serve, slice the Hempnut-Crusted Tofu Steaks in half. Arrange the Jalapeño-Agave Succotash in the center of a serving plate. Place the tofu steaks over the succotash and drizzle the kecap manis over them.

Noodulars

Here's a challenging section of this cookbook. Noodles are not just noodles. Noodles are Noodular at The Galaxy Global Eatery. We've taken the best of the best from past menus, and started with a basic pasta recipe that incorporates hemp flour without offending the Italian side of my family. Here it is necessary to start with the egg base from which all pasta originates. A little bit of everything for everyone. We have not limited ourselves to Italian pasta. We have chosen Noodular dishes that come from the far reaches of China, Laos, and Japan in our effort to offer a global range to choose from when you're planning your next hemp picnic. Grandmothers love the Mascarpone Hemp Lasagna Rolls. Tradition can always be enhanced with hemp. One of my favorites is the Udon Hempesto. On a sunny day, the color of chlorophyll with udon noodles can't be beat! Don't forget to create a romantic mood by setting the table with the finest hemp linen and beeswax candles made from hempseed oil. Locate Way Out Wax Company in Vermont for your hemp candle needs. Tell 'em you heard about them in The Galaxy.

Hemp Pasta

Serves 6

> 3/4 cup semolina flour (unbleached white flour can be substituted)
> 1/4 cup hemp flour
> 1 teaspoon salt
> 5 egg yolks
> 2 tablespoons hempseed oil
> water to bring dough together

Combine the semolina and hemp flours and salt in a large bowl. Make a well in the center of the flour mix and add beaten yolks and hempseed oil. Mix in by hand or with a mixer. Let the yolks and oil incorporate until the mixture has a sandy texture. Add water (1 tablespoon at a time) until the dough comes together. Knead for about 8 minutes, until dough is leathery. If the dough is sticky, knead in more flour. Allow the dough to sit for 45 minutes. Follow pasta machine maker's instructions for specific pasta type desired. Cook fresh pasta in salted water for 4 to 5 minutes. You may substitute dry pasta for any of the noodle dishes in this section and cook for 7 to 8 minutes, following the instructions on the pasta box.

Hemp Pasta

with Apple Cider-Braised Autumn Vegetables

SERVES 6

Hemp Pasta
Follow pasta machine maker's instructions to successfully make linguine using the recipe on page 156.

Apple Cider-Braised Autumn Vegetables
      1 carrot, peeled and diced
      1 parsnip, peeled and diced
      1 zucchini, diced
      2 tablespoons butter
      1 apple, peeled and diced
      1 tomato, diced
    $1/4$ cup apple cider
      salt and pepper to taste

Dice the vegetables to a uniform size. (It is important that all vegetables are the same size to facilitate proper cooking.)

Add 1 tablespoon of butter to a sauté pan and melt. Add carrots and parsnip and cook over a medium-low heat for 5 minutes. Add zucchini and apple and cook an additional 3 minutes. Add tomato, apple cider, and remaining butter and cook until the apple cider has reduced by half. Season with salt and pepper to taste.

To serve, toss the Hemp Pasta with the Apple Cider-Braised Autumn Vegetables and serve in a bowl.

Calabasa Soba Noodles
with Spicy Kaffir Lime-Ginger Broth & Hemp Green Sauce

SERVES 6

Spicy Kaffir Lime-Ginger Broth
          1 tablespoon sesame oil
          3–4 slices ginger, about the size of a quarter
          1 tablespoon garlic, minced
          3–4 Thai peppers
          12 cups water
          1 cup miso (approximately) (see Glossary)
          3–4 kaffir lime leaves, cut chiffonade (see Glossary)
          splash of fresh-squeezed lime juice

Heat sesame oil in a large pot and sauté ginger, garlic, and Thai peppers until the garlic is golden. Add water, enough miso so its taste is detectible, lime leaves, and lime juice. Heat until hot but not boiling.

Hemp Green Sauce
          1/2 cup ginger, sliced
          1/2 cup scallions, minced
          1/8 cup hempseed oil
          1/2 cup peanut oil
          salt and pepper to taste

Combine the ginger and scallions in a food processor or blender until processed to a coarse mince. Add the hempseed and peanut oils and continue to blend until smooth. Add salt and pepper to taste.

Calabasa Soba Noodles

    3 12-ounce packages soba noodles
    6 tablespoons peanut oil
    6 tablespoons garlic, minced
    1 pound mushrooms, sliced
    1 pound calabasa, boiled until tender but firm
    4^1/$_2$ cups Spicy Kaffir Lime-Ginger Broth
    6 tablespoons Hemp Green Sauce
    6 tablespoons scallions, chopped, for garnish

Set a pot of water to boil. When the water is boiling, drop in the soba noodles. Allow to cook for 2 minutes, or until the noodles are cooked but still firm. Pour into a colander and run under cold water. Warm the peanut oil in a skillet, then add garlic and mushrooms and cook until the mushrooms are soft. Add the cooked calabasa and toss in to the mix. Add the drained noodles and continue to mix well.

To serve, mound the noodle mixture in the center of a deep bowl. Ladle the Spicy Kaffir Lime-Ginger Broth over the noodles and spoon the Hemp Green Sauce on top. Garnish with scallions.

Somen Noodles
with Hempnut Tahini

SERVES 6

Hempnut Tahini

    2 tablespoons peanut oil

    1/2 cup shallots, minced

    1/4 cup garlic, minced

    1/3 cup fresh ginger, minced

    3/4 tablespoon dried ginger

    1/2 cup hempnuts

    3/8 cup water

    1 cup white wine

    1/8 cup rice wine vinegar

    1 1/2 tablespoons sesame oil

    1/2 cup scallions, sliced

    salt and pepper to taste

Heat the peanut oil in a sauté pan. Add the shallots, garlic, fresh ginger, dried ginger, and hempnuts. Sauté for about 2 minutes. Add water to deglaze, then remove the sauce from the heat.

Bring the white wine to a boil in a separate pot and add sautéed ingredients along with the rice wine vinegar, sesame oil, and scallions. Simmer until syrupy and season with salt and pepper to taste.

Somen Noodles

  18 ounces somen noodles (see Glossary)
  $^1/_2$ cup peanut oil
  1 cup onion, diced
  $^3/_8$ cup light soy sauce
  $^1/_2$ cup Hempnut Tahini
  1 cup mung beans (see Glossary)
    salt and cayenne pepper to taste
  1 teaspoon sesame seeds for garnish

Put a pot of water to boil, then add the somen noodles. Cook for 1 to 2 minutes, until cooked but still firm. Drain and set aside. Heat the peanut oil and sauté the onion until soft. Add the soy and Hempnut Tahini sauces. Add the cooked somen noodles to the mixture and toss well. Add mung beans and toss for another 30 seconds. Add salt and cayenne pepper to taste.

To serve, place the Somen Noodles in the center of a serving plate and sprinkle generously with sesame seeds.

Eating hempseed fortifies the basic defense systems of the human body. Essential fatty acids clean out arterial cholesterol buildup from saturated fats, and reduce the risk of heart attack.—Dr. Roberta Hamilton, Professor Emeritus, UCLA, Los Angeles, CA, 1991

Udon Hempesto

    2 tablespoons butter or vegetable oil
    3 garlic cloves, minced
    2 scallions, thinly sliced
    3 ears corn
    3 roasted red peppers, chopped
    3 roasted poblano peppers, chopped
    1 recipe Hempesto (page 162)
   18 grape tomatoes
    1 cup Vegetable Stock (page 7)
    3 pounds fresh udon noodles (see Glossary)
      salt and pepper to taste
    6 ounces fresh mozzarella, cut into $1/2$-inch cubes (optional)

Melt the butter in a medium pan and sauté the garlic and scallions until the garlic is slightly golden. Shuck the ears of corn and blanch the corn cobs. Allow them to cool, then remove the kernels. Add the corn kernels, red peppers, and poblano peppers and sauté for 1 minute. Add the Hempesto and tomatoes and cook on medium until all are combined and almost brought to a boil. Add the Vegetable Stock and cook for 1 minute. Add salt and pepper to taste.

Meanwhile, bring a pot of water to a boil and cook the udon noodles for 30 seconds. Drain. Transfer noodles to the sauce and mix.

Garnish with the fresh mozzarella. Serve.

Greek Hempesto Linguini

Serves 6

Hemp Pasta

1 recipe Hemp Pasta (page 156)
3/4 cup Kalamata olives, pitted
2 cups grape tomatoes

Follow pasta machine maker's instructions to successfully make linguine using the recipe on page 156. (Use packaged dry pasta as a substitute.)

Hempesto

1 bunch fresh basil
1/4 cup hempnuts, toasted
1 garlic clove
2 tablespoons feta cheese, grated
1/4 cup hempseed oil
1/2 cup extra virgin olive oil
salt and pepper to taste

The best way to make pesto is to use a mortar and pestle and slowly incorporate all pesto ingredients. An easier way to make pesto is to use a blender. Place basil, hempnuts, garlic, and feta cheese in blender and puree. Slowly add the hempseed and olive oils with the blender running on a low speed. Season with salt and pepper to taste.

To serve, pit the olives and wash the tomatoes. Place the pasta in salted boiling water and cook until tender (al dente). Drain water and add Hempesto, olives, and tomatoes. Season with salt and pepper to taste.

Pumpkin Hemp Dumplings
with Chinese Black Vinaigrette

SERVES 4

Pumpkin Hemp Dumplings

1 pound pumpkin, cubed

1/2 cup water

1-inch piece ginger, grated

2 tablespoons heavy cream

2 tablespoons hempseed oil

1 teaspoon sesame oil

1/4 cup scallions, chopped

salt and pepper to taste

12 square wonton wrappers

2 eggs, beaten, for egg wash (see Glossary)

Clean and deseed the pumpkin. Cut the flesh into 2-inch cubes. Place the pumpkin cubes and water in a pot and cook slowly until all the water has evaporated (about 30 minutes). Add the ginger and cream. Reduce to low heat and cook until all the liquid has evaporated. The consistency should be like mashed potatoes. Put the mixture in blender and puree. While the blender is on, slowly add hempseed and sesame oils. Then add the scallions and season with salt and pepper to taste. Refrigerate until cold.

Boil the wonton wrappers in lightly-salted water. Cook 3 to 4 skins at a time for about 30 seconds. Remove to an ice bath and spread out on parchment paper with a little oil to avoid drying.

Beat the eggs with water to make an egg wash (see glossary) in a stainless steel bowl. Place a little less than a teaspoon of the dumpling mixture in the center of each wonton. Brush the edge of the wonton skins with egg wash. Fold the wontons over and seal the edges together with your fingers. Repeat until all wontons are filled and sealed.

→

Chinese Black Vinaigrette

    1 teaspoon peanut oil

    2 garlic cloves, chopped

    1/2 cup sweet black vinegar

Add the peanut oil to a hot pan. Sauté the garlic until it begins to turn golden. Add the black vinegar.

To prepare, heat the Chinese Black Vinaigrette to a boil and add the Pumpkin Hemp Dumplings. The vinaigrette will start to thicken and form a glaze over the dumplings. Season with salt and pepper to taste. Drizzle the remaining sauce over the dumplings and serve.

Buddha was nourished with Hemp Seed

Many Buddhist traditions, writings, and beliefs indicate that Siddhartha, the Buddha, used and ate nothing but hemp and its seeds for six years prior to discovering his truths and becoming the Buddha.

Hempnut Ravioli

with Shiitake Mushroom, Kale, & Broccolini Filling & Sage-Orange Hemp Butter Sauce

SERVES 6

Shiitake Mushroom, Kale, & Broccolini Filling

        1 pound Hemp Cheese (page 5)
        1 egg
      3/4 cup parmesan cheese
        6 kale leaves, chopped
        1 cup broccolini, chopped
      1/2 cup rehydrated shiitake mushrooms, thinly sliced
        2 tablespoons hempseed oil
          salt and pepper to taste

In a bowl mix all ingredients together until well blended.

Hempnut Ravioli

        1 pound unbleached white flour
        5 eggs, plus 1 additional egg yolk
      1/2 cup hempnuts
        1 egg and 1/2 egg shell of water for egg wash

Mound the flour on a clean, smooth surface. Make a well in the center of the mound and add the 5 whole eggs and additional yolk. Work the flour and eggs together with a fork, a little at a time, until all flour has been absorbed. Add the hempnuts and knead to even consistency. Make a thin sheet by rolling out the pasta until it is approximately 1/8-inch thick. Cut the sheet into two equal halves.

Place one half of the rolled out pasta sheet on a large working surface. Place teaspoons of filling 1 inch apart on the pasta sheet until you have used up all the filling. Beat egg with water to make egg wash and brush around each filling. Lay the other half of the pasta sheet on top and press down on the spaces surrounding the filling to seal each ravioli. Cut individual ravioli squares and place them on a floured cookie sheet.

→

Sage-Orange Hemp Butter Sauce

> 1 cup Hemp Butter (page 4)
>
> 1 cup unsalted butter
>
> 18 sage leaves
>
> zest and juice from 1 orange
>
> 2 cups boiling Vegetable Stock (page 7)
>
> parmesan for garnish
>
> hempnuts for garnish
>
> salt and pepper to taste

Place the hemp and unsalted butter in a sauté pan. Add the sage leaves, zest, and juice. As the butter begins to boil, add the boiling Vegetable Stock. Emulsify and sprinkle in the parmesan cheese and hempnuts. Add salt and pepper to taste.

To prepare, cook the Hempnut Ravioli in salted boiling water until just tender (about 1 minute). Pour Sage-Orange Hemp Butter Sauce over the ravioli and serve.

Hempnut Mushroom Ravioli
with Beet & Fennel Garnish

SERVES 4

Hemp Pasta

> 1 recipe Hemp Pasta (page 156)

Ravioli Filling

> 2 portobello mushrooms
>
> 2 tablespoons olive oil
>
> 1/4 cup heavy cream
>
> 2 thyme sprigs
>
> 2 tablespoons brandy
>
> 1 egg for egg wash (see Glossary)
>
> salt and pepper to taste

Clean the portobello mushrooms by scraping and discarding the black gills from the caps. Cut the mushrooms into strips, including the cleaned stem. Heat the olive oil over high heat in a sauté pan. Once the pan begins to smoke, add mushrooms and sauté for 2 minutes. Add the cream and thyme sprigs. Let the cream reduce by half before adding the brandy. Reduce for an additional 2 minutes over low heat. Puree in a blender until smooth. Season with salt and pepper to taste and reserve in refrigerator. Place one half the rolled out pasta sheet on a large working surface. Follow instructions for Hempnut Ravioli (page 167).

Beet & Fennel Garnish

> 1 beet
> 1/2 fennel bulb
> 2 tablespoons olive oil
> 1 garlic clove, chopped
> 1/4 pound spinach
> salt and pepper to taste
> 2 tablespoons butter for finishing

Bake the beet in a 400°F oven for 1 hour, or until tender. Slice beet into 1/2-inch cubes. Set aside. Cut fennel into 1/2-inch cubes and toss with 1 tablespoon olive oil, salt, and pepper. Place the fennel on a cookie sheet and roast for 12 minutes.

Heat a sauté pan over high heat. Add the remaining oil and cook garlic until browned, then add the spinach. Wilt the spinach thoroughly. Season with salt and pepper.

To prepare, cook the Hemp Mushroom Ravioli in boiling salted water for about 2 minutes. Drain. Place spinach in the center of the plate, and top with the ravioli. Melt butter until it foams up and turns slightly brown. Pour over the ravioli. Serve the Beet and Fennel Garnish on top.

Spinach-Walnut Hemp Manicotti
with Eggplant Puree

SERVES 4

Hemp Pasta

1 recipe Hemp Pasta (page 156)

Make pasta dough and roll out to the #1 setting on your pasta machine, or roll out manually to a 1/8-inch thickness. Cut into 5- x 7-inch rectangles and keep covered and refrigerated.

Filling

1 tablespoon vegetable oil
1 small garlic clove, chopped
1 pound spinach
3/8 cup walnuts
2 tablespoons hempseed oil
1/2 cup cream cheese
1/4 cup heavy cream
1 tablespoon fresh basil, thinly sliced

Heat the vegetable oil over medium-high heat. Add chopped garlic, spinach, and walnuts and sauté for about 1 minute, until the spinach has wilted. Place the mixture in blender and puree. Place pureed mixture in a bowl. Incorporate the hempseed oil, cream cheese, and heavy cream. Wash, dry, and thinly slice the basil leaves. Mix the basil into the other ingredients and set aside.

Eggplant Puree

> 1 medium eggplant
> 1/2 cup olive oil
> 8 garlic cloves
> 2 thyme sprigs
> salt and pepper to taste

Peel eggplant and cut into cubes. Add the eggplant, olive oil, whole peeled garlic cloves, and thyme sprigs to a medium saucepan. Let the mixture slowly simmer over medium-low heat for about 20 minutes. The garlic should be soft and light brown. If the garlic begins to burn it should be discarded. Allow the mixture to cool for 30 minutes, then puree in a blender until velvety smooth. Season with salt and pepper to taste and set aside.

To prepare, cook Hemp Pasta sheets in salted boiling water for about 1 to 2 minutes. Remove from water and pat dry. Roll the heated spinach mixture in the pasta rectangles to form Spinach-Walnut Hemp Manicotti. Repeat until all are rolled and the filling is used up. Heat the Eggplant Puree to slightly warmer than room temperature and pour over the manicotti. Serve.

One acre of hemp produces as much paper as 4.1 acres of trees over the same 20-year period.

Mascarpone Hemp Lasagna Rolls
with Tomato Sauce

SERVES 6

Lasagna Rolls

2 tablespoons hempseed oil

3 leeks, diced

3 garlic cloves

1 pound mascarpone cheese

$^1/_2$ pound ricotta cheese

$^1/_2$ pound shiitake mushrooms

2 tablespoons olive oil

10 basil leaves, thinly sliced

$^1/_4$ cup hempnuts, toasted

10 asparagus stalks

12 lasagna sheets

2 pounds spinach leaves

Heat the hempseed oil on low heat. Cook the leeks and garlic until tender. Allow to cool to room temperature, then add the mascarpone and ricotta cheese. Sauté the shiitake mushrooms in 1 tablespoon of olive oil over high heat. Allow to cool, then add to the cheese mixture.

Preheat oven to 375°F.

Add the basil and the toasted hempnuts to the cheese mixture. Cook the asparagus in salted boiling water for 1 to 2 minutes. Remove to an ice bath. Cut the stalks into thirds. Use the same boiling water to cook the lasagna sheets as per the manufacturer's instructions.

Spread the cheese mixture over half of one lasagna sheet. Place 5 pieces of asparagus over the cheese so that it hangs over the edge of the pasta by at least 1 inch. Roll the lasagna into small cylinders, like jellyrolls. Stand the rolls upright so the asparagus sticks out on one side. Continue with remaining lasagna sheets. Place lasagna rolls in the oven for 4 to 5 minutes.

Tomato Sauce

  1 medium Spanish onion, diced
  3 garlic cloves, chopped
  1/2 teaspoon fennel seed
  2 tablespoons olive oil
  1 bay leaf
  1 16-ounce can plum tomatoes
  1 tablespoon tomato paste
    salt and pepper to taste

Over medium-low heat, slowly cook the onion, chopped garlic, and fennel seed in the olive oil. Once the onion is translucent and fennel seed is fragrant, add the bay leaf, canned tomatoes, and tomato paste and simmer for 40 minutes. Season with salt and pepper to taste and set aside.

To serve, heat the remaining olive oil in a pan over a high flame. Cook the spinach leaves until wilted. Arrange the spinach on a serving plate and lean 3 Mascarpone Hemp Lasagna Rolls against the spinach with the asparagus pointing upwards. Ladle the Tomato Sauce next to them.

Hempnut Chestnut Gnocchi

SERVES 6

> 2 pounds Idaho potatoes
> 1 1/2 cups unbleached white flour
> 2/3 cup chestnut flour
> 2 eggs
> 1/2 cup parmesan cheese, freshly grated
> 1 teaspoon ground nutmeg
> 2 tablespoons hempnuts
> salt and pepper to taste
> 1 recipe Hemp Marinara (page 81)

Boil the potatoes in a pot of salted water until tender (about 10 to 12 minutes). Peel the potatoes and pass them through a food mill. Mound the mashed potatoes on a clean work surface and make a well in the center. Combine all the remaining ingredients (except the Hemp Marinara) and place them in the well. Mix everything together until it forms a homogenous dough. Knead the dough until it is smooth. If it is sticky, add a little more flour.

Divide the dough into 4 equal portions and roll each portion into a 1/2-inch wide log. Cut the log into 1-inch pieces of gnocchi. Shape each gnocchi into oval shapes and roll each one along the backside of a fork to create grooves. Place the gnocchi on a floured tray as you roll them.

Cook the Hempnut Chestnut Gnocchi in a large pot of boiling salted water until they float (3 to 4 minutes), then lift them out gently with a slotted spoon. Mix with the Hemp Marinara sauce and serve.

Hemp Cheese Gnocchi
with Hemp Curry Sauce

SERVES 4

Hemp Curry Sauce

$1/2$ small yellow onion, diced

1 garlic clove, minced

$1/4$ cup hempseed oil

2 tablespoons red curry (see Glossary)

1 teaspoon cumin powder

1 cup Hemp Milk (page 4)

$1/2$ cup Hemp Cheese (page 5)

3 garlic cloves, blanched three times

salt and pepper to taste

Sweat the onion and minced garlic in 2 tablespoons of the hempseed oil. Add the curry and cumin and cook, stirring constantly, for 2 minutes. Place the mixture in blender with Hemp Milk, Hemp Cheese, and blanched garlic.

(To blanch the garlic, put a small pot of water to boil. Add the desired amount of garlic cloves and boil for about 5 minutes. This process softens the intense flavor of raw garlic.)

Puree the mixture thoroughly in a blender. Slowly add the remaining hempseed oil until an emulsion forms. Season with salt and pepper to taste.

Hemp Cheese Gnocchi

1 pound Hemp Cheese (page 5)

1 egg

1 cup unbleached white flour

1 teaspoon salt

1 tablespoon peanut oil

1 pound spinach

2 cups cherry tomatoes

Combine Hemp Cheese and egg together and mix by hand. Slowly add the flour until it becomes a bit sticky but does not stick to your fingers. Use both hands

to roll the dough into a cylinder shape, about 1 inch in diameter. Cut into 1-inch pieces. Put a pot of water to boil. Add the salt and cook the raw gnocchi until they float. Set aside.

To prepare, heat the peanut oil in a medium pan and sauté the spinach and the tomatoes. Ladle the Hemp Curry Sauce onto a serving plate. Mix the Hemp Cheese Gnocchi with the spinach and tomatoes and arrange on top of the sauce. Serve.

Hempnut Spätzle
with Roasted Vegetables & Apricot-Infused Oil

SERVES 8

Hempnut Spätzle
    2$^{1}/_{8}$ cups unbleached white flour
    $^{1}/_{2}$ cup hemp flour
    1 cup water
    $^{1}/_{2}$ cup whole milk
    $^{1}/_{2}$ cup water
    5 eggs
    $^{1}/_{4}$ cup hempnuts
    1 teaspoon nutmeg
    salt and pepper to taste

Mix all the ingredients together. Put a pot of salted water to boil. Use a baker's spatula and a spätzle maker (see Glossary) or ricer to push the dough through the holes into the boiling water. Cook until firm (about 1 to 2 minutes), scoop out with a spider (see Glossary), and run under cold water to prevent over-cooking. To serve, sauté with a touch of butter and salt and pepper to taste.

Roasted Vegetables

    1 yellow squash, $1/2$-inch dice

    1 zucchini, $1/2$-inch dice

    1 small white onion, $1/2$-inch dice

    2 Japanese eggplants, $1/2$-inch dice

    1 red pepper, $1/2$-inch dice

    1 poblano pepper, $1/2$-inch dice

    $1/2$ cup olive oil

    5 garlic cloves, minced

    salt and pepper to taste

    1 cup balsamic vinegar

    $1/4$ cup sugar

Preheat oven to 400°F. Toss all the vegetables in olive oil, garlic, salt, and pepper and lay out on a sheet pan or baking pan. Bake in the oven for 30 minutes. Meanwhile, reduce the balsamic vinegar and sugar by half. Toss the roasted vegetables with the balsamic reduction. Set aside.

Apricot-Infused Oil

    1 cup apricot juice

    $1/2$ cup peanut oil

Boil the apricot juice in a small pot until reduced by three-fourths. Place the juice in a blender with the oil and blend until emulsified. Use or store in the refrigerator for up to two weeks.

To serve, place the Roasted Vegetables in the center of a serving plate. Position the Hempnut Spätzle around the vegetables and drizzle the Apricot-Infused Oil on top.

Tofu Balls

with Green Pasta & Roasted Pepper Sauce

SERVES 6

Roasted Pepper Sauce

18 large red peppers
1 medium red onion
1/4 cup olive oil
1/4 cup hempseed oil
salt and pepper to taste

Rub the peppers with a little olive oil and turn over an open flame or under a broiler. Scorch the skin, then remove to a bowl and cover with plastic wrap. Once cooled, peel, seed, and chop the peppers. Puree the peppers with the raw red onion in a food processor or blender. Add the olive and hempseed oils with the blender on a slow speed. Season with salt and pepper to taste.

Tofu Balls

4 slices dry bread
1 cup canned black beans
1 pound firm tofu
1 tablespoon olive oil
1 tablespoon garlic, minced
3/4 cup white onion, minced
1 tablespoon ginger, minced
1 teaspoon ground cumin
2 tablespoons miso paste (see Glossary)
1/2 cup carrots, sliced julienne
salt and pepper to taste
1/4 cup coconut oil or other high-temperature frying oil

Grind the dry bread to a coarse bread crumb in a food processor. Transfer to a bowl and set aside. Mash the black beans and transfer to the bowl of bread crumbs. Crumble the tofu into the bowl and mix. Heat the olive oil and sauté the garlic, onion, and ginger until translucent. Add the cumin, miso paste, and carrots.

Cook for 2 minutes and add to the bowl. Mix the ingredients together with your hands until well combined. Add salt and pepper to taste. The mixture should be stiff enough to form small balls. If not, add some more bread crumbs. Form the mixture into $1^1/2$-inch balls. Heat the coconut oil and fry the tofu balls until golden brown. Set aside.

Green Pasta

> 2 pounds spinach pasta
> 4 tablespoons sesame oil
> $3/4$ cup scallions, minced
> 24 Tofu Balls
> 3 cups Roasted Pepper Sauce
> 6 tablespoons parmesan, grated

Cook pasta in boiling salted water until al dente. Drain and set aside. Heat the sesame oil in a sauté pan. Add 2 tablespoons of the chopped scallions and the meatballs and cook until heated through. Add the pasta and toss with the Roasted Pepper Sauce for 30 seconds to 1 minute.

To serve, place the Green Pasta and Tofu Balls in a bowl. Spoon the Roasted Pepper Sauce around the pasta and garnish with the remaining scallions and parmesan cheese.

 The original draft of the Declaration of Independence was written on hemp paper.

Laotian Spring Salad

SERVES 6

Noodles

> 17 ounces vermicelli noodles

Put a pot of water to boil. Cook the noodles per directions on the package (approximately 5 to 7 minutes), until al dente.

Dressing

> 2 cups rice wine vinegar
> 3/8 cup Thai chili sauce
> 2 tablespoons cilantro, chopped
> 2 teaspoons sugar
> 1/4 cup Nam Pla fish sauce (see Glossary)
> 2 tablespoons ginger, chopped
> 3 tablespoons garlic, chopped
> 2 jalapeño peppers, chopped
> 3 cups olive oil
> 1 cup hempseed oil
> salt and pepper to taste

Mix the vinegar, chili sauce, cilantro, sugar, fish sauce, ginger, garlic, and jalapeño peppers. Whisk the mixture together and slowly add the olive and hempseed oils to form an emulsion. Add salt and pepper to taste.

Vegetables

        1 cucumber, sliced julienne
        1 green pepper, sliced julienne
        1 red pepper, sliced julienne
        1 red onion, sliced julienne
        1 asparagus stalk, cut 1-inch dice
        1 bunch scallions, thinly sliced
     18 grape tomatoes, cut in halves
   1/3 cup cilantro leaves
        black sesame seeds for garnish

Mix all the vegetables together with the noodles in a stainless steel bowl. Add the dressing and toss. Place the salad in a deep bowl, sprinkle with black sesame seeds, and serve.

The Old Dutch Masters Painted on Hemp Canvas

Hemp is the perfect archival medium. The paintings of Van Gogh, Gainsborough, and Rembrandt were primarily painted on hemp canvas.

Fish, Meat, & Poultry

Without a doubt this was the most controversial chapter of the book. Do we or don't we include fish, meat, and poultry? The question haunted us for months. But finally we decided to be true to The Galaxy Global Eatery's mission statement: not only do we provide innovative foods for progressive palates, but we are a "Love All, Serve All" establishment. My personal beliefs notwithstanding, it's likely that some of you eat fish, meat, and poultry, and some of these dishes happen to be favorites among our clientele. Here we need to state that if meat is to be part of the diet, we strongly encourage nothing but organic, free-range meat and poultry. As for fish, we don't support the sale of swordfish, cod, Chilean sea bass, or other fish that are in danger of over exploitation. Line-caught or farm-raised fish are preferred. The continuing debate about the necessity of animal protein for a wholesome diet is ongoing at The Galaxy Global Eatery and is still unresolved. I personally believe that a vegetarian diet with a strong emphasis on "Living Foods" is the most desirable. But again, for the purposes of this cookbook, we want to encourage as wide an audience as possible to incorporate hemp into their diet. We believe that hemp nuts, seeds, oil, and flour play a wonderfully complementary role in our fish, meat, and poultry dishes. As long as strict guidelines regarding food sources are adhered to, these recipes will offer something unique and delicious. So for all you carnivores and fish enthusiasts, here is a small, well-chosen selection for you—because we love you too.

Pumpkin Macau

Serves 6

              6 baby pumpkins, tops cut off, seeds removed
              4 tilapia filets, cut into chunks
              1 potato, thinly sliced
              3 red peppers, sliced
              1 large red onion, sliced
              3 plum tomatoes, sliced
          1 1/2 cans coconut milk
              2 tablespoons minced garlic
              1 tablespoon chili flakes
              1 tablespoon Vegetable Stock (page 7)
              2 tablespoons agave nectar (see Glossary)
              2 tablespoons salt
            12 cilantro sprigs
              2 tablespoons hempseed oil

Preheat oven to 400°F.

In a large bowl, combine all ingredients except the cilantro and hempseed oil. Stuff the pumpkins equally and put the tops back on. Place in oven and bake until pumpkins are tender, about 30–45 minutes. Garnish with the cilantro and hempseed oil. Serve with a spoon.

Pistachio Hempnut-Crusted Sea Bass
with Persimmon-Ginger Sauce & Stir-fried Watercress

MAKES 6

Pistachio Hempnut-Crusted Sea Bass

6 6-ounce filets sea bass
$1/2$ cup clarified butter (see Glossary)
   salt and cayenne pepper to taste
1 cup hempnuts
1 cup pistachios, crushed
2 tablespoons peanut oil

Preheat the oven to 450°F. Rub the sea bass filets with clarified butter so that the nuts will stick. Salt and pepper the filets. Mix together the hempnuts and pistachio nuts in a stainless steel bowl. Dredge the fish in the nut mix until coated. Heat the peanut oil in a nonstick frying pan. Sauté the fish on both sides until golden brown (about 4 minutes per side). Transfer the sea bass to an oven-safe pan and cook in the oven for an additional 5 to 8 minutes, depending on the thickness

Persimmon-Ginger Sauce

$1/2$-inch piece ginger, peeled and minced
1 tablespoon butter
$1/2$ cup fresh-squeezed orange juice
3 persimmons, washed and pureed
2 tablespoons fresh-squeezed lime juice
   salt and pepper to taste

Sauté the ginger in a tablespoon of butter. Add the orange juice, persimmons, and lime juice. Simmer for 5 minutes. Season with salt and pepper to taste. Set aside.

Stir-fried Watercress

> 6 tablespoons Vegetable Stock (page 7), or water
>
> $1/2$ teaspoon brown sugar
>
> 2 tablespoons soy sauce
>
> 1 tablespoon sesame oil
>
> 2 tablespoons peanut oil
>
> 2 tablespoons garlic, minced
>
> 2 tablespoons ginger, minced
>
> 3 bunches fresh watercress, rinsed with hard ends clipped off

Mix the Vegetable Stock, brown sugar, soy sauce, and sesame oil in a small bowl. Heat a wok or deep frying pan and add the peanut oil, garlic, and ginger. Fry for 1 minute. Add the watercress and fry for an additional 30 seconds, or until watercress is bright green. Add the Vegetable Stock-soy sauce mixture and stir until mixed.

To serve, arrange the Stir-fried Watercress on one side of a large serving plate. Ladle the Persimmon-Ginger Sauce opposite it. Position the sea bass over the sauce.

 Hempseed oil is used in laundry detergents that biodegrade naturally in our water systems.

Hempnut-Crusted Catfish Filets

with Citrus Couscous & Pomelo, Avocado, & Asparagus Salsa

SERVES 6

Hempnut-Crusted Catfish Filets

      6 7-ounce filets catfish
  1/2 cup clarified butter (see Glossary)
      salt and cayenne pepper to taste
  1/4 cup hempnuts
    1 tablespoon vegetable oil
    1 recipe Lemon-Ginger Hemp Aioli (page 79) to finish

Rub the catfish filets with clarified butter so that the hempnuts will adhere. Season with salt and cayenne pepper to taste and dredge the fish in hempnuts until coated on all sides. Add the vegetable oil to a smoking-hot pan. Sear the catfish and cook until flaky (about 5–8 minutes).

Citrus Couscous

    1 tablespoon vegetable oil
    1 small white onion, chopped
    1 pound couscous (see Glossary)
    2 cups cranberry juice
    1 cup fresh-squeezed orange juice
  1 1/2 cup water
    2 pieces star anise
    2 tablespoons butter
  1/2 bunch scallions, chopped

Heat the vegetable oil in a saucepan and sauté the chopped onion. Once the onion is translucent, add the couscous and stir until coated with oil. Add the cranberry and orange juices, water, and star anise. Mix thoroughly, then cover the pan and turn the heat down to medium-low. Once the couscous has absorbed the water, stir in the butter and scallions. Set aside.

→

Pomelo, Avocado, & Asparagus Salsa

    1 avocado
    1 pomelo or grapefruit
    10 asparagus stalks
    1 tablespoon vegetable oil

Peel and dice avocado. Peel, segment, and dice pomelo or grapefruit and add to the diced avocado. Place the asparagus in salted boiling water for 1¹/₂ minutes, then remove to an ice bath. Once cold, dice, add to the avocado mixture, and toss with vegetable oil.

To serve, place a serving spoonful of Citrus Couscous in the center of a serving plate. Place 1 Hempnut-Crusted Catfish Filet over the couscous. Sprinkle more hempnuts over the catfish. Ladle the Pomelo, Avocado, & Asparagus Salsa over the fish and serve. Serve with Lemon-Ginger Hemp Aioli.

Maple Hempnut-Crusted Salmon
with Sautéed Summer Vegetables

SERVES 4

Maple Hempnut-Crusted Salmon

    4 7-ounce salmon filets
      salt and pepper to taste
    1 tablespoon vegetable oil
    ¹/₄ cup maple syrup
    ¹/₄ cup hempnuts

Season the salmon filets with salt and pepper. Add the vegetable oil to a smoking-hot sauté pan. Place the salmon filets, skin-side down, in the oil and reduce heat to medium-low. As the skin side is cooking, brush maple syrup on the flesh side. Allow salmon to cook for about 5 to 6 minutes, until only the top is still raw. Rub the hempnuts into flesh side of the salmon. The maple syrup will act as an adhesive for the hempnuts. Turn salmon flesh-side down and cook an additional 2 minutes.

Sautéed Summer Vegetables

    3 medium red potatoes
    3 tablespoons vegetable oil
       cumin to taste
       salt to taste
    3 garlic cloves
    2 medium zucchini
    2 medium yellow squashes
    3 plum tomatoes
    1/4 pound sugar snap peas

Slice the red potatoes into 1/4-inch rounds. Add 1 tablespoon of the vegetable oil to sauté pan and heat until smoking. Add the potatoes, cumin, and salt, and turn the flame down to medium-low heat. Turn the potatoes over as soon as they are golden brown in color. Remove from the pan.

Slice the garlic into very thin slivers and set aside. Wash the zucchini and yellow squash. Slice into 1/4-inch rounds. Heat a sauté pan over high heat and add 2 tablespoons of vegetable oil. Sauté the zucchini, yellow squash, and garlic for about 3 minutes, turning the vegetables, until they are golden-brown around the edges. Season with cumin and salt and set aside.

Dice the plum tomatoes and set aside. Boil the sugar snap peas in salted water. Cook for 2 minutes and remove to an ice bath.

To serve, place all vegetables into a sauté pan to reheat. Arrange the Sautéed Summer Vegetables in alternating colors on a serving plate. Place the Maple Hempnut-Crusted Salmon over the vegetables.

Five Spice Salmon
with Asian Egg Noodles & Hemp Cilantro Pesto

SERVES 6

Hemp Cilantro Pesto

$1/4$ cup hempnuts

$1/4$ cup cashews

4 bunches fresh cilantro

$1/4$ cup parmesan

$1/4$ cup hempseed oil

$1/4$ cup extra virgin olive oil

salt and pepper to taste

1 small poblano pepper

Blend all ingredients until smooth. Refrigerate or set aside for serving.

Asian Egg Noodles

3 packages thin Asian egg noodles

1 cucumber, peeled and cut julienne

$1/2$ pound snow peas, washed and cut julienne

2 bunches scallions, washed and thinly sliced on a bias

salt and pepper to taste

water to boil noodles

Boil the noodles in a large pot and cook for approximately 4 to 6 minutes. Strain and run cold water through the pasta. Allow to cool. Mix the noodles with the cucumber, snow peas, and half the scallions. Mix in the Hemp Cilantro Pesto. Season with salt and pepper to taste and place in a large bowl. Refrigerate until ready to serve.

Five Spice Salmon

            2 pounds boneless salmon filet
              salt and pepper to taste
            8 ounces Chinese five spice (see Glossary), for blackening
            3 tablespoons peanut oil
              chopped scallions for garnish

Season the salmon filets with salt and pepper. Rub the five spice all over the salmon until well coated. Heat the peanut oil in a frying pan. Add the salmon and cook to medium doneness, or until just becoming flaky (about 5 minutes). Place in the refrigerator uncovered until completely cool. Divide the filet into 6 portions.

To serve, mound the Asian Egg Noodles in a serving bowl and place a piece of the Five Spice Salmon on top. Garnish with a small mound of chopped scallions.

Hempseed oil is a preferred base for house paints.

Mini-Mango Shrimp Spring Rolls
with Hemp Curry Sauce

SERVES 4

Mini-Mango Shrimp Spring Rolls

1 mango, thinly sliced

$1/2$ cup daikon radish, thinly sliced

1 cup (25–30) tiger shrimp, shelled and deveined

1 teaspoon ginger, grated

2 teaspoons sesame oil

2 tablespoons soy sauce

3 cups coconut oil or other high-temperature frying oil

12 spring roll wrappers (see Glossary)

Slice the mango and daikon radish into spaghetti-thin strands. Each strand should be approximately 2 inches long. Set them aside in a bowl. Clean the shrimp and add to the bowl. Add the ginger, sesame oil, and soy sauce. Mix together and refrigerate to marinate for 30 minutes. Drain excess liquid.

Heat the coconut oil in a deep saucepan and bring it to 350°F. Cut the spring roll wrappers in half. Place the filling inside each wrapper and slowly roll, making sure to tuck in the edges. Sprinkle a little water on the edge to facilitate the sealing and finish rolling. Continue until all the spring rolls are filled. Deep-fry the spring rolls 3 or 4 at a time until golden brown (about 4 minutes). Remove to paper towels to drain excess oil.

Hemp Curry Sauce

4 tablespoons green Thai curry paste (see Glossary)

$3/4$ cup soy sauce

$1/4$ cup hempseed oil

$1/3$ cup rice wine vinegar

Whisk together all ingredients.

To serve, ladle the Hemp Curry Sauce on the center of a serving plate. Stack 3 Mini-Mango Shrimp Spring Rolls rolls in the center of the sauce.

Spicy Shrimp Escabeche

<small>SERVES</small> 4

1 pound medium shrimp
1 teaspoon red pepper flakes
1 bay leaf
1 small red onion, diced
1 yellow pepper, diced
3 tablespoons hempseed oil
1 tablespoon coriander seeds
5 tablespoons fresh-squeezed lime juice
3 tablespoons capers
1 bunch cilantro
1 teaspoon Thai chili paste

Peel and devein the shrimp. Add the red pepper flakes and bay leaf to salted simmering water. Add the shrimp and cook for $1^1/2$ minutes, or until translucent. Remove the shrimp to an ice bath to stop the cooking process.

Add the raw red onion and yellow pepper to the drained cooked shrimp.

Place a small pan over low heat and add hempseed oil and coriander seeds. Toast them for approximately 3 minutes and add to shrimp. Add the lime juice, capers, and whole washed cilantro leaves. Add the Thai chili paste to taste. (Each type of chili paste has a varying degree of spiciness. Add 1 teaspoon at a time as a guideline.) Refrigerate for at least 30 minutes before serving.

Cilantro Shrimp Salad

SERVES 6

1 pound medium shrimp, diced
1-inch piece ginger, grated
3 Thai chilies, chopped
1 tablespoon garlic, chopped
1 tablespoon sugar
2 tablespoons Nam Pla fish sauce (see Glossary)
1 medium red onion, diced
4 baby bok choy (see Glossary)
2–3 green papayas
1/2 bunch cilantro
3 tablespoons peanut oil
2 tablespoons hempseed oil
1/2 cup hempnuts, toasted
2 scallions, chopped
1/4 cup peanuts, toasted

Clean and devein the shrimp. Dice each shrimp into 4 equal pieces. Set aside.

Combine the grated ginger, Thai chilies, garlic, sugar, Nam Pla fish sauce, and red onion. Whisk together and set aside to use as marinade. (Marinade should be added to the shrimp 30 minutes prior to cooking.)

Add the washed and halved baby bok choy to salted boiling water for 3 minutes. Remove to an ice bath until cold, then set aside. Peel and deseed the green papaya and shred or cut into fine slivers. Pick and wash the cilantro leaves and set aside. Heat a frying pan over medium-high heat until it smokes. Add the marinated shrimp and cook for 2–3 minutes, or until translucent.

Add the peanut and hempseed oils, toasted hempnuts, scallions, and cilantro leaves and continue to cook for 1 minute.

To serve, arrange the green papaya and baby bok choy on a serving plate. Place the Cilantro Shrimp Salad in a mound on top. Sprinkle with toasted peanuts to garnish.

Sugar Cane Grilled Jumbo Shrimp
with Hempnut Black Rice Cakes & Orange-Fennel Aioli

SERVES 6

Hempnut Black Rice Cakes

> 2 tablespoons butter
> 1 cup black rice
> 3 cups water
> 1/4 cup pickles, chopped
> 1/2 cup panko bread crumbs (see Glossary)
> 1/2 can chipotle peppers, pureed
> salt and pepper to taste
> unbleached white flour for dredging
> 2 eggs for dredging
> hempnuts for dredging
> 4 tablespoons peanut oil

Heat the butter in a pot, then add the black rice and stir until the rice is well coated with butter. Add the water and bring to a boil. Once it reaches the boiling point, stir well and reduce to a simmer. Cover and cook for 30 minutes. Allow the rice to overcook until it becomes soft and sticky. Set aside to cool. Add the chopped pickle, bread crumbs, and pureed chipotle to the rice. Add salt and pepper to taste.

Make 12 rice cakes of equal size. Place the flour, eggs, and hempnuts in 3 separate bowls. Dredge the rice cakes by first covering them in flour, then in egg, and then in hempnuts.

Heat the peanut oil in a sauté pan and fry the rice cakes until golden brown. Transfer to paper towels to absorb excess oil. Keep warm in the oven until serving.

→

Sugar Cane Grilled Jumbo Shrimp

12 jumbo shrimp

juice from 6 sour oranges

2 tablespoons fresh thyme leaves

1 tablespoon raw cane sugar

$1/2$ cup olive oil

salt and pepper to taste

Peel and devein the jumbo shrimp, leaving the tails intact. Mix the orange juice, thyme leaves, cane sugar, olive oil, and salt and pepper in a bowl. Place the shrimp in a container and marinate in the refrigerator for 30 minutes to 3 hours. Once the other ingredients are prepared, heat the grill or BBQ. Grill until marked on all sides and the shrimp are firm but tender.

Orange-Fennel Aioli

4 cups fresh-squeezed orange juice

$1/2$ tablespoon fennel seed

2 egg yolks

$1 1/2$ cups peanut oil

salt and pepper to taste

Boil the orange juice with the fennel seed in a small pot and reduce until it becomes a syrup. Allow to cool. In a stainless steel bowl, add egg yolks to the orange reduction and beat with a whisk. Add the peanut oil slowly, in a steady stream, continuing to beat vigorously until a mayonnaise forms. Add salt and pepper to taste.

Garnish:

$1/2$ bulb fennel, shaved very thin

18 orange segments

To serve, place the shaved fennel in center of a serving plate. Put a dollop of Orange-Fennel Aioli at 2 o'clock, 6 o'clock, and 10 o'clock. Place 2 Hempnut Black Rice Cakes over the fennel. Lean 2 Sugar Cane Grilled Jumbo Shrimp up against the rice cakes. Arrange 3 orange segments next to each dollop of aioli.

Chipotle Chili Mussels

SERVES 6

    6 tablespoons garlic, thinly sliced
    4 shallots, minced
      zest of 4 oranges
    8 tablespoons canned chipotle chilies, minced
    3 tablespoons olive oil
    6 pounds mussels, washed
    8 tablespoons fresh-squeezed orange juice
    3 tablespoons hempseed oil
  24 cilantro sprigs
    6 Hemp Rolls (page 229)
    1 recipe Orange Hemp Aioli (page 76)

Sauté the garlic, shallots, orange zest, and chipotle chilies in olive oil in a deep frying pan on high heat for 2 minutes. Add the mussels and orange juice.

Cover the pan and steam the mussels until they open. (Discard any unopened mussels.)

Serve Chipotle Chili Mussels with the cooking liquid in a deep dish. Garnish with the cilantro, hempseed oil, and a few dollops of Orange Hemp Aioli. Serve with Hemp Rolls.

Hempnut-Crusted Lamb Chops
with Buckwheat-Beet Salad & Mint Salsa

SERVES 6

Buckwheat-Beet Salad

2 beets

$1/2$ cup water

3 tablespoons olive oil

1 Spanish onion, diced

1 cup whole grain buckwheat kernels

$2 1/2$ cups boiling water

1 bay leaf

1 thyme sprig

salt to taste

2 tablespoons butter

$1/8$ teaspoon black pepper

Preheat oven to 400°F. Clean the beets and sprinkle them with salt, then place in a casserole dish. Add $1/2$ cup of water and cover the dish with aluminum foil. Place the beets in the preheated oven for approximately 50 minutes (time will vary depending on size of beets). Once cooked through, peel and slice them into $1/4$-inch rounds. Heat olive oil in a saucepan and add diced onion. Once onion becomes translucent, add the buckwheat and stir. Add the boiling water, bay leaf, thyme sprig, and salt. Cover the pot and place it over medium-low heat. Cook until just tender (about 15 minutes). Stir in the butter and black pepper. Mix all the ingredients together and set aside.

→

Mint Salsa

    12 sun-dried tomatoes
     1 head garlic, roasted
     1 medium red onion, roasted
     1 thyme sprig
     1 tablespoon olive oil
     2 poblano peppers
     3 tablespoons fresh mint leaves, sliced
    1/4 teaspoon ground cumin
     2 tablespoons red wine vinegar
     1 tablespoon hempseed oil

Rehydrate the sun-dried tomatoes by covering them in warm water for 30 minutes. Then chop them into sixths and set aside. Slice away the root of the garlic head. Thinly slice the red onion. Place the garlic, onion, and thyme sprig on a sheet of aluminum foil. Drizzle with 1 tablespoon of olive oil and fold up the edges like an envelope surrounding the contents. Roast in the preheated oven (it's okay to cook these while the beets for the salad are cooking) for 20 to 30 minutes. Remove once the garlic cloves are soft. Place the poblano peppers directly on the burner. Turn on the flame and allow the skin to blister on all sides. Remove to a bowl and cover with plastic wrap. Allow the peppers to steam for 20 to 30 minutes. Once cooled, peel and dice them into 1/2-inch squares. Add the sliced mint to the sun-dried tomatoes. Add cumin, red wine vinegar, and hempseed oil. Mix all the ingredients well and set aside.

Hempnut-Crusted Lamb Chops

        18 2-ounce lamb chops
        $1/8$ teaspoon kosher salt
        $1/8$ teaspoon black pepper
        1 tablespoon olive oil
        2 tablespoons Dijon mustard
        $1/2$ cup hempnuts

Preheat the oven to 400°F. Season the lamb chops with salt and pepper. Add the olive oil to a smoking-hot pan. Sear both sides of the chops until golden brown (not cooked through). Brush the lamb chops with Dijon mustard and then encrust them by covering both sides thoroughly with hempnuts.

Prepare the lamb chops by cooking them in a 400°F oven an additional 6 to 7 minutes, depending on the thickness.

To serve, place 3 beet rounds on each serving plate. Place a spoonful of the Buckwheat-Beet Salad in the center of each plate. Lean the Hempnut-Crusted Lamb Chops against the salad and spoon the Mint Salsa over the lamb chops.

Francis Scott Key wrote the first verse of the Star Spangled Banner on a Hemp envelope.

I am prepared to deliver . . . hemp to your port, watered and prepared according to the Act of Parliament.—George Washington, in a 1765 letter

Apricot-Glazed Hemp Pork Loin
with Roasted Garlic Sweet Potatoes & Steamed Baby Bok Choy

SERVES 4

Apricot-Glazed Hemp Pork Loin

> 2 pounds pork loin
> salt and pepper to taste
> 2 tablespoons olive oil
> 1/2 cup apricot preserves
> 3 tablespoons champagne vinegar
> 1/2 cup hempnuts

Preheat the oven to 400°F. Season the pork loin with salt and pepper. Add olive oil to a smoking hot pan. Place the pork loin in pan and sear both sides. Transfer the loin to an oven-safe pan and continue to cook in the oven for 20 minutes. Whisk the apricot preserves and champagne vinegar in a metal bowl. Remove pork from oven and brush with apricot glaze. Sprinkle with hempnuts and cook in the oven for an additional 3 minutes. Remove the pork from the oven and allow it to sit for 5 minutes before slicing.

Roasted Garlic Sweet Potatoes & Steamed Baby Bok Choy

2 pounds sweet potatoes
1 head garlic
3 tablespoons olive oil
1/4 cup light brown sugar
1 teaspoon pure vanilla extract
4 tablespoons butter
4 heads baby bok choy (see Glossary)

Preheat the oven to 400°F. Peel the sweet potatoes and place them in a pot of boiling water. Cook until tender. Drain and set aside.

Cut and remove the root from the head of garlic. Place the garlic on a sheet of aluminum foil and fold up the edges. Add a tablespoon of olive oil, seal, and roast in the oven for about 30 minutes. The roasted garlic should be soft, slightly brown, and very aromatic. Remove the cloves from their skins and set aside.

Add the sweet potatoes, roasted garlic, brown sugar, vanilla, and butter to a food processor. Puree until smooth, then season with salt.

Place the baby bok choy in a steamer over salted boiling water for 2 minutes, or until tender. Remove to an ice bath and set aside.

To serve, place portions of Roasted Garlic Sweet Potatoes and Steamed Baby Bok Choy side by side. Shingle the sliced Apricot-Glazed Hemp Pork Loin around the edges.

Herodotus described Scythians purifying and cleansing themselves with hempseed oil, which "makes their skin shining and clean."—Herodotus, *Histories IV*, 450 B.C. University Press, Cambridge, MA. 1906, pp. 74–76

Hempnut Bison Tamale

with Stuffed Poblano Peppers & Tangy Fruit Salsa

SERVES 6

Tamale Filling

    1 pound bison meat (London broil or any better cut desired)

    3 tablespoons butter

    3 tablespoons olive oil

    2 garlic cloves, minced

    1 small onion, minced

    1 leek, white part only, thinly sliced

    2 small zucchini, diced

    2 small bananas, diced

    $1/3$ cup mixed currants and dates, minced

    1 teaspoon cayenne pepper

    $1/2$ teaspoon cinnamon

    $1/4$ teaspoon ground cloves

    2–4 cups Vegetable Stock (page 7)

    1 teaspoon fennel seeds, crushed

    3 tablespoons herbs (cilantro, parsley, sage), minced

    salt to taste

Cut the bison meat into small cubes. Warm the butter and oil together until hot. Sauté the garlic, onion, and leek stalk until golden. Add the bison and cook until until seared on all sides (about 2 minutes). Add the zucchini, bananas, currants, dates, cayenne pepper, cinnamon, cloves, and 2 cups of Vegetable Stock. Simmer for 15 to 20 minutes to reduce, adding more stock as necessary. When the mix has reduced by half add the fennel seeds and herbs. Season with salt. Continue to reduce and replenish with Vegetable Stock until the bison and zucchini are tender (about 5–8 minutes).

→

Tamale Dough

1 small onion, diced

1/2 red bell pepper, minced

2 garlic cloves, minced

2–2 1/2 cups Vegetable Stock (page 7)

1 1/2 cups whole milk, warm

2 tablespoons hempseed oil

salt and pepper to taste

4 1/2–5 cups masa harina (see Glossary)

12 dried or fresh corn husks (soak for 30 minutes if dry)

Combine the onions, red bell pepper, garlic, Vegetable Stock, milk, hempseed oil, and salt and pepper. Use a wooden spoon to stir in the masa harina, forming the mixture into a soft, thick, pliable dough. (Add more masa harina or stock if the dough is too wet or too dry.) Cover the dough with plastic wrap and let sit for 15 to 30 minutes. Take a soaked corn husk and open it in the palm of your hand. Spread 1 1/2 tablespoons of the dough into the open husk. Place 2 teaspoons of filling in the center of the dough. Fold one side of the husk over the top, and then the other side. Tie the top end together with a piece of husk. Fold the bottom end underneath. Repeat for each tamale. Place them in a steamer and steam for 1 hour, or until firm.

Stuffed Poblano Peppers

8 poblano peppers

3 medium ears corn, roasted and shucked

1/2 cup sharp white cheddar cheese, grated

3 scallions, trimmed and minced

1 garlic clove, minced

1/4 cup cilantro, minced

3 tablespoons currants

salt and pepper to taste

3/4 cup dry bread crumbs

1/4 cup blue cornmeal

1 cup unbleached white flour for dredging

3 egg whites, lightly beaten

Preheat the oven to 400°F. Roast the poblano peppers over an open flame until charred. Place them in a bowl and seal with plastic wrap. Allow to steam until cooled. Peel the peppers, being careful not to remove the stem. Set aside 6 peppers to be stuffed. Core, seed, and cut the flesh of 2 of the poblano peppers into small pieces. Grill the ears of corn and remove the corn kernels. Place in a bowl with the cheddar cheese, scallions, garlic, cilantro, and currants. Season with salt and pepper to taste and mix the ingredients well. Make a lengthwise incision down each remaining pepper, taking care not to tear the skin. Scrape out the core and seeds. Stuff each pepper with the corn mixture. Combine the bread crumbs and cornmeal. Dredge each pepper by dipping each one first in the flour, shaking off the excess, then in the egg whites, and then in the bread crumb mixture. Place them on a nonstick baking sheet. Bake in the preheated oven for 20 minutes, or until hot and golden.

Tangy Fruit Salsa

>   1 mango, peeled, seeded, and diced
>   2 cups blueberries, washed
>   4 strawberries, diced
>   1/2 avocado, diced
>   1 teaspoon garlic, minced
>   1 tablespoon agave nectar (see Glossary)
>   1 tablespoon fresh-squeezed lime juice
>   1 teaspoon red chili flakes

Mix all ingredients and set aside.

To serve, place a Stuffed Poblano Pepper in the center of each serving plate. Place 2 Hempnut Bison Tamales on either side of the pepper. Spoon Tangy Fruit Salsa around the tamales.

Hempnut Fried Chicken

SERVES 6

3 whole chickens, quartered
3 cups bread crumbs
1 cup hempnuts
2 tablespoons cayenne pepper
2 tablespoons salt
2 tablespoons cajun spice
1 tablespoon powdered garlic
3 cups unbleached white flour for dredging
8 eggs, beaten for dredging
coconut oil or other high-temperature frying oil

Wash the chicken and pat dry.

Mix the bread crumbs, hempnuts, cayenne pepper, salt, cajun spice, and powdered garlic in a stainless bowl. Place the flour and the eggs in 2 separate bowls.

Dredge the chicken in flour, then the eggs, and then the bread crumb-hempnut mix.

Preheat the oven to 250°F. Heat the oil in a deep pot to 350°F. Fry each piece of chicken in the hot oil until golden brown. Transfer to paper towels to absorb excess oil. Keep the chicken warm in the oven until all pieces are fried and ready to serve.

Duck Confit Salad

with Raspberry Vinaigrette

SERVES 4

Duck Confit

> 6 duck legs
> 1 head garlic, cut in half
> 2 oranges, cut in half
> 6 cups rendered duck fat (see Glossary)
> 20 black peppercorns
> 1 bay leaf
> 2 rosemary sprigs
> 2 thyme sprigs
> 2 cloves
> 6 juniper berries

Preheat oven to 350°F. Place the duck legs in a casserole dish. Place the halved garlic head and oranges, skin and all, in the casserole dish. Pour in the rendered duck fat to completely cover the duck legs. Arrange the peppercorns, bay leaf, rosemary, thyme, cloves, and juniper berries around the duck legs. Place the casserole dish over medium heat. Once the fat begins to simmer, cover dish with aluminum foil and place in preheated oven. Cook for about 2 hours. The duck meat should be very tender and should fall off the bone.

Raspberry Vinaigrette

       2 tablespoons hazelnut oil
       1 tablespoon hempseed oil
       1 shallot, chopped
       2 garlic cloves, chopped
       1/4 cup hazelnuts
       1 cup raspberries
       1 orange, segmented
          salt and pepper to taste
       1 cup watercress
       2 tablespoons hempnuts, toasted

Heat the hazelnut and hempseed oils over medium-low heat. Add the chopped shallots and garlic. Once the shallots are translucent, add the hazelnuts, raspberries, and segmented orange. Cook an additional 2 minutes. Season with salt and pepper to taste.

To serve, place the washed and dried watercress in metal bowl and toss with the Raspberry Vinaigrette. Place the salad in the center of plate and lean the Duck Confit against the salad. Sprinkle with hempnuts. Spoon any remaining dressing over duck legs.

Clinical use of Ma Zi (hempseed plant) extends deep into ancient Chinese Medicine. A major section of the great pharmacopoeia of China, the Pen T'sao Kang Mu, was devoted exclusively to hempseed.
—Kenneth Jones, *Nutritional and Medicinal Guide to Hemp Seed*, 1995

Bakery

Some people might think of this section as the "no-brainer" section of a hemp cookbook due to the fact that most recipes ever written with hemp ingredients are for baked goods. I beg to differ as it is my opinion that this is the most exciting area of hemp cuisine. We meticulously tested these recipes for content and style in order to present a truly culinary section for the baker of hemp foods. And a winner it is. From basic Hemp Dinner Rolls, to Hemp Java Dipping Sticks, to Hemp Maize Bread for your southern dinner buffet, to Galaxy's world-renowned Hemp-Crusted Apple Pie and scrumptious Key Lime Pie—you won't be disappointed. And we haven't forgotten the vegans out there . . . try Virgo's Vegan Carrot Cake. For something a little lighter, settle by the fireplace with a Hemp Chai Tea and a basket of Hemparoons. Life is sweet! Enjoy.

Curry-Turmeric Hempnut Sticks

MAKES 2¹/₂ DOZEN

2 cups unbleached white flour
1¹/₂ teaspoons baking powder
1 teaspoon curry powder (see Glossary)
¹/₄ teaspoon turmeric
¹/₂ teaspoon salt
3 tablespoons solid vegetable shortening
¹/₂ to ³/₄ cup ice water, ice cubes removed
¹/₂ cup toasted hempnuts
2 tablespoons hempseed oil
coarse salt

Preheat oven to 350°F. Using a food processor fitted with metal blade, pulse a few times to combine flour, baking powder, curry, turmeric, and salt. Add the shortening and pulse 8 to 10 times until mixed to the consistency of coarse meal. With the machine running, gradually add ice water until a dough ball forms. You may not need all the water. Make sure the dough does not become sticky.

Spread the hempnuts on a work surface. Transfer the dough on top of hempnuts and smooth with your fingers into a 4 x 6 rectangle. Use a rolling pin to roll the rectangle into an 8 x 10 rectangle, ¹/₄-inch thick. Flip the dough so that both sides are completely coated with hempnuts. Use a pizza cutter or long sharp knife to cut the dough lengthwise into ¹/₄-inch-long strips.

Roll each strip into a 16-inch rope between palm of your hand and a flat rough surface, like a plastic or wood cutting board. (This facilitates rolling dough studded with hempnuts.) Place the dough sticks on an ungreased baking sheet, pressing the ends down slightly to keep from shrinking during baking. Brush each strip gently with hempseed oil and sprinkle with coarse salt. Bake 14 to18 minutes in the preheated oven. Remove the sticks to a wire rack to cool completely. Store in airtight containers.

Hemp Java Dipping Sticks

MAKES ABOUT 3 DOZEN

> 2 cups all-purpose flour
> 1/2 cup hemp flour
> 1 teaspoon baking powder
> 1 cup sugar
> 4 tablespoons (1/2 stick) unsalted butter, softened
> 2 large eggs
> 2 teaspoons pure vanilla extract
> 1/3 cup pine nuts
> 3 tablespoons hempnuts, toasted
> 1 teaspoon whole anise seed

Preheat the oven to 350°F. Grease a baking sheet and set aside.

Combine the all-purpose and hemp flours with the baking powder in a medium mixing bowl.

In a large bowl, with an electric mixer on high, beat the sugar and butter together until the mixture is light and airy (about 3 to 4 minutes). Add the eggs one at a time, beating until combined after each addition. Add the vanilla. With the mixer on low, add the pine nuts, hempnuts, and anise seed and beat until just combined. Add the flour mixture and beat until just combined and a dough begins to form. Divide the dough in half.

Form each half into a flattened log 4 inches wide and 1/2-inch thick. Place them about 3 inches apart on the greased baking sheet.

Bake for 20 to 25 minutes, or until firm to the touch and lightly golden on the edges. Remove from oven, leaving oven on, and let cool on baking sheet for 5 minutes. Transfer to a cutting board with a large spatula. Using a serrated bread knife, cut each log crosswise and at a slight angle into 1/2-inch slices. Lay slices flat on baking sheet and continue to bake until they look lightly toasted (10 to 12 minutes more). Use a spatula to transfer to a wire rack to cool completely. Store in airtight containers.

Hempnut Bread Twists

MAKES 1 DOZEN

> 1/4 cup warm water (105–115°F)
> 1 3/4 teaspoons dry active yeast
> 4 1/2 cups unbleached white flour
> 2 teaspoons salt
> 1 1/4 cups cool water
> 1/2 cup hempnuts, toasted
> 1/4 cup hempseed oil
> coarse salt

Combine the warm water and yeast in a small bowl. Let sit for 5 minutes, or until creamy. Combine the flour and salt in a large bowl and form a well. Add the yeast mixture along with the cool water. Mix until a sticky dough forms. Turn the dough out onto a lightly-floured surface and knead for 4 minutes. The dough should still be sticky and not smooth. Knead in additional cool water by the tablespoonfuls if dough feels stiff or dry. Place the dough in a lightly-floured bowl. Cover with plastic wrap and allow to sit for 20 minutes.

Return the dough to a lightly-floured surface and knead for another 8 minutes. The dough will become smooth and supple. Place the dough in an oiled bowl and cover again with plastic wrap. Allow the dough to rise at room temperature for 1 hour. Punch the dough down and pat into a 12-inch square. Sprinkle the dough lightly with 1/3 of the toasted hempnuts. Fold the dough into thirds, like a business letter, to make a 12- x 4-inch rectangle. Gently pinch the ends to seal. Spray the dough generously with water. Coat both sides of dough with remaining hempnuts. Gently brush both sides with hempseed oil and sprinkle with coarse salt.

Place the dough on a lightly-oiled baking sheet. Cover with plastic wrap and allow to rise in the refrigerator for 40 minutes. Return the dough to a lightly-oiled work surface. Use a pizza cutter or long sharp knife to cut the dough crosswise into 12 1-inch wide strips. Lift each strip, stretching it slightly, then twist it around like coil and place it on a lightly-oiled baking sheet. Repeat with remaining strips, placing them side by side with no space between them. Cover with plastic wrap and allow to rise at room temperature for about 30 minutes. →

Meanwhile, preheat the oven to 425°F. Put an empty pan on the baking shelf below where the bread will be placed. After rising is complete, place the twists in the oven and quickly pour 1 cup of hot water into the empty pan. Shut the oven door. Wait 1 minute, then open the over door only long enough to spray a mist of water several times over the twists. Mist again after another minute. Bake the twists for 15 minutes. Reduce the oven temperature to 375°F and bake an additional 10 minutes, or until the twists look golden brown and sound slightly hollow when tapped. Transfer to a wire rack to cool at least 15 minutes before serving. Completely cooled bread can be sealed tightly and frozen.

Additional fillings:
(Add ingredients along with the hempnuts when sealing the dough into thirds.)
      pitted and chopped olives
      chopped fresh herbs such as rosemary, thyme, & basil
      dried fruits like currants, cherries, cranberries, dates, or apricots

In the writings of ancient physician Claudius Galen (130–200 A.D.), he mentions a cannabis seed dessert that was popular with the Romans.

Mexicali Hempnut Cheese Crackers

MAKES ABOUT 5 DOZEN

> 2 cups jalapeño jack cheese, grated
> 4 tablespoons ($1/2$ stick) unsalted butter, softened
> 1 cup all-purpose flour
> $1/4$ cup hemp flour
> $1/4$ cup hempnuts, toasted
> 2 tablespoons fresh cilantro, chopped
> $1/4$ teaspoon salt
> whole cilantro leaves for garnish

In a large mixing bowl with an electric mixer on high, beat together cheese and butter until softened and well blended (about 2 minutes). Add all-purpose and hemp flours, hempnuts, cilantro, and salt. Beat until just combined. Do not overbeat. If dough does not come together, add 1 or 2 tablespoons of water. Knead the dough 2 or 3 times to thoroughly blend all ingredients. Divide into 2 equal balls. Roll each ball into a $1^1/2$-inch thick log, 6 inches long. Wrap in plastic and refrigerate at least 30 minutes, or up to 24 hours.

Preheat oven to 350°F. Slice the logs into rounds a little less than 1 inch thick. Place cracker rounds on an ungreased baking sheet. Gently press a whole cilantro leaf into center of cracker. Bake 12 to 15 minutes, until edges are golden. Cool on a wire rack. Store in tins at room temperature for up to 3 days, or refrigerate in plastic for up to 2 weeks.

Toasted Hempnut Cracker Crisps

MAKES ABOUT 12 DOZEN

$^1/_2$ cup hempnuts, toasted
4 teaspoons salt
$2^1/_2$–$2^3/_4$ cups all-purpose flour
$^1/_2$ cup hemp flour
1 teaspoon salt
$1^1/_2$ cups warm water
hempseed oil for brushing

Stir together the toasted hempnuts and 4 teaspoons of salt. Set aside. Place the all-purpose and hemp flours and remaining teaspoon of salt in a food processor fitted with a metal blade. Pulse for a few seconds to combine. With the machine running, slowly add the water in a steady stream until a ball of dough forms. If it does not form because the dough is too sticky, add more flour and process to form a ball. If it is too dry, add 2 to 3 tablespoons more water with the motor running.

Remove ball of dough to a lightly-floured surface and knead for about 1 minute. Place the dough in a bowl and cover with plastic wrap. Allow to sit at room temperature for 30 minutes.

Preheat oven to 500°F. Position a rack in center of oven. Have 2 baking sheets ready, along with a spray bottle filled with water.

Cut the dough into 8 equal pieces. Work with one piece at a time while keeping the remaining dough covered with plastic wrap. Press a piece of dough onto a lightly-floured work surface to flatten it. Use a rolling pin to roll the dough into a large thin rectangle of even thickness, dusting with flour if dough is too sticky. Gently roll the dough up and around the rolling pin to transfer it onto one of the ungreased baking sheets. Brush off any additional flour. Brush a thin coating of hempseed oil over the sheet of dough.

Use a pizza cutter or a sharp knife to cut the dough into cracker-sized rectangles. Do not try to separate them, as this will occur naturally during baking. Sprinkle evenly with 1 heaping tablespoonful of the hempnut mixture. Spray lightly with water.

Bake for 2 to 3 minutes. Open the oven and remove any crackers that have started to brown with a spatula. Return the pan to the oven and continue baking, checking every 30 seconds until all the crackers are golden. Remove the crackers to a wire rack, breaking apart any that did not separate during baking. Some will be crispy already, while others will become crispy during cooling. Continue rolling, seasoning, and baking the remaining dough pieces.

Store cooled crackers in tins or in tightly-sealed plastic bags for up to 1 month.

Fried Hempnut Crisps

Makes 2–3 dozen

$1/2$ cup hempnuts
2 whole eggs
unbleached white flour for sprinkling (about 1 cup)
3 cups peanut oil (for frying)
salt and pepper to taste

Combine the hempnuts and eggs in a small bowl, then sprinkle 3 tablespoons of white flour at a time over the mix. Use your hands to combine the mixture until it just comes together. The mixture should not be wet. If necessary, add a little more flour. Transfer the dough ball to a lightly-floured work surface and roll it out with a rolling pin to a $1/8$-inch thickness. Using a paring knife, cut it into long thin triangles.

Heat the peanut oil in a medium saucepan. Place the strips in the oil one at a time. Fry for 2 to 3 minutes, until golden brown. Season with salt and pepper to taste and remove to paper towels to absorb excess oil. Serve.

Cumin Hempnut Soft Pretzels

MAKES 16 PRETZELS

    2 cups warm water
    1 2-ounce package dry active yeast
4³/4 cups bread flour
    2 tablespoons ground cumin
    2 teaspoons salt
    6 tablespoons (³/4 stick) unsalted butter, cut into small pieces
    1 tablespoon hot pepper sauce
    2 tablespoons cornmeal
12 cups water
    2 tablespoons baking soda
    1 teaspoon sugar
    1 teaspoon salt

Egg Wash

    1 egg yolk
    1 tablespoon water
    coarse salt
    hempnuts

Combine the warm water and yeast in a small bowl. Allow to sit for 5 minutes, until creamy. Combine the flour, cumin, and 2 teaspoons of salt until well blended. Use a pastry blender or two knives to cut the butter into the flour mixture until coarsely blended to a coarse meal.

Form a well in center of flour mixture. Pour in proofed yeast and hot pepper sauce and mix to form a sticky dough. Turn the dough out onto floured work surface. Knead the dough until smooth and slightly sticky, adding more flour by the tablespoonfuls if very sticky (about 8–10 minutes). Form the dough into a ball and place in a large buttered bowl. Cover with plastic wrap and allow to sit at room temperature for 30 minutes, or until doubled in volume.

Punch down the dough. Knead for an additional 1 to 2 minutes, until smooth. Divide the dough in half, and then divide each half into 8 equal parts to total 16 pieces (each about the size of a golf ball). Place the dough pieces on a sheet pan and cover with a towel. Work with one piece of dough at a time. Roll each piece between the palms of your hands and the table into a rope about 20 to 24 inches long. Shape each rope into pretzel form and place it on a baking sheet that has been sprinkled with cornmeal. Keep the pretzels covered with a towel. Repeat with the remaining dough pieces. Let shaped pretzels sit for 20 minutes, or until doubled in size.

Meanwhile, preheat oven to 375°F and bring the 12 cups of water to a boil in a large wide saucepot. Add the baking soda, sugar, remaining teaspoon of salt, then reduce to a simmer. Transfer the pretzels to the simmering water a few at a time with a large spatula. Simmer about 30 to 40 seconds per side. Remove the pretzels to a heavily-buttered cookie sheet. Brush each pretzel with the egg wash and sprinkle generously with coarse salt and hempnuts. Repeat with remaining pretzels, working in batches if necessary.

Bake for 20 minutes, rotating the baking sheets from the top to bottom shelves and moving them from the back to the front halfway through baking time. Remove to wire racks to cool. Serve warm or at room temperature. Pretzels are best when eaten the same day they are made. Freeze or wrap tightly in aluminum foil to store.

 The fiber composite industry is the largest potential market for hemp fibers.

Hemp Dinner Rolls

MAKES 1 DOZEN ROLLS

> 1 2-ounce package quick rising yeast
> 2 cups warm water
> 1/3 cup agave nectar (see Glossary)
> 1 tablespoon salt
> 1/4 cup hempseed oil (plus more for brushing)
> 4 1/2 cups bread flour
> 1/2 cup hempnuts
> 1/2 cup hemp flour

Mix the yeast with warm water. Stir in the agave nectar and wait for 15 minutes, until the mixture foams. If it does not foam, start again with fresh yeast.

Add salt and hempseed oil to the yeast. Combine half of the bread flour with the mixture.

Add the hempnuts, hemp flour, and the remaining bread flour and knead for about 10 minutes. When the dough is smooth and soft (not sticky) place it in a bowl and proof (allow the dough to rise for 40 minutes).

Preheat the oven to 375°F.

Form the dough into 2-inch roll-shaped balls. Place them on a baking sheet and brush with the extra hempseed oil. Make an "X" mark on the top of each roll and allow to proof again for an additional 15 minutes.

Bake the rolls for 15 minutes, or until golden brown. Allow to cool for 5 minutes before serving.

Indian Spiced Chapati or Roti

SERVES 4–5

>   3/4 cup unbleached white flour
>   1/4 cup hemp flour
>   1 teaspoon kosher salt
>   1/2 cup tepid water (see Glossary)
>   2 teaspoons hempseed oil
>   2 teaspoons cumin
>   2 teaspoons hempnuts
>   1 teaspoon ground coriander

Combine unbleached white flour, hemp flour, and salt in medium bowl.

Form a well in the center. Pour the water and hempseed oil into the well and slowly combine all the ingredients. The mixture should be somewhat wet and sticky. Add the cumin, hempnuts, and coriander.

Turn out onto a lightly-floured work surface and knead for 8 minutes. The dough should become more leathery as it is kneaded. Allow the dough to rest for about one hour.

On a floured work surface, roll out the dough to about 1/4-inch thick.

Heat a cast-iron pan until it just begins to lightly smoke. Place the dough in the pan and cook for about 2 minutes. Turn it over and cook an additional 2 minutes. Both sides should be equally browned.

Brush the finished chapati with hempseed oil. Wrap them in aluminum foil or towels until ready to serve.

Hempnut Pita

MAKES 8

2^1/$_2$ cups warm water
1 tablespoon sugar
3^1/$_2$ tablespoons active dry yeast
4^1/$_2$ cups unbleached white flour
1 cup hemp flour
^{1}/$_2$ tablespoon salt
^{1}/$_2$ teaspoon hempseed oil
^{1}/$_2$ cup hempnuts

Preheat oven to 500°F.

Combine the water, sugar, and yeast in large bowl. Allow to sit for 5 minutes. In a separate bowl, mix the white and hemp flours and salt. Add to the yeast mixture, starting with 3^1/$_2$ cups flour, then gradually adding the rest. Stop adding flour when the dough no longer sticks to the side of the bowl, but use enough flour to keep it from sticking.

Knead well for 5 minutes. Put the hempseed oil on the palms of your hands and smooth all over dough to prevent crusting. Cover with plastic wrap or a cotton towel. Allow to proof for 30 minutes.

Divide dough into 8 equally-sized balls. Roll out each ball into ^{1}/$_4$-inch thick round. Allow to sit covered for 20 minutes on a well-floured counter top. Bake on ungreased baking sheets for 5 to 8 minutes, or until lightly browned. Hempnut Pitas may be kept in a plastic bag in the refrigerator for several days or frozen in airtight bags, but are best eaten hot out of the oven.

Rosemary Hempnut Focaccia

MAKES 1 FOCACCIA

Focaccia

3$^{1}/_{2}$ cups unbleached white flour

1 cup warm water

1$^{1}/_{2}$ teaspoons dry active yeast

1$^{1}/_{3}$ cups baked potato, finely grated and lightly packed

2 tablespoons hempseed oil

1$^{1}/_{4}$ teaspoons coarse salt

Topping

2 tablespoons hempseed oil

2 tablespoons chopped fresh rosemary leaves

1$^{1}/_{4}$ teaspoons coarse salt

$^{1}/_{4}$ cup hempnuts

Use a standing mixer to combine $^{1}/_{2}$ cup of the flour, $^{1}/_{2}$ cup of the warm water, and all of the yeast to form a spongy dough. Cover the dough tightly with plastic wrap and allow to sit at room temperature for 30 minutes.

Add the remaining flour, warm water, baked potato, hempseed oil, and coarse salt. Use the mixer's paddle attachment and mix on low speed until the dough comes together. The dough should be sticky (this is good because the wet dough will help form air pockets and add chewiness). Switch the mixer to a dough hook attachment and increase the speed to medium. Continue kneading the dough this way until smooth, elastic, and slightly sticky (about 5 minutes). Transfer the dough to a lightly-oiled bowl, turning it to coat with oil; then cover tightly with plastic wrap. Allow to rise at room temperature for 1$^{1}/_{2}$ hours, or until the dough has doubled in volume.

Note: If mixing by hand, add remaining flour, etc., and mix with wooden spoon until a sticky dough forms. Turn onto a lightly-floured surface and knead about 10 minutes, adding additional flour by the tablespoonfuls if necessary, until smooth, elastic, and slightly sticky. Be careful not to add too much additional flour. The dough should be sticky to help form the proper texture when baked. Transfer to a lightly-oiled bowl and continue as above.

Use your wet hands to punch down the dough. Generously coat a 15-x10-inch pan with hempseed oil. Press the dough into pan, filling all the way into the corners as best as possible. If the dough is too elastic, cover it with plastic wrap and allow to sit for 15 minutes, then try again. Cover the dough with oiled plastic wrap and allow to rise at room temperature for about 1 1/2 hours, or until puffy and doubled in volume.

Meanwhile, adjust the oven rack to the lower middle position and preheat the oven to 425°F. With two wet fingers, dimple the risen dough at regular intervals to prepare for the toppings. Drizzle 2 tablespoons of hempseed oil over the dough and sprinkle evenly with the rosemary leaves, salt, and hempnuts. Bake for 23 to 25 minutes, or until focaccia is golden brown and crisp. Remove from pan and transfer to wire rack to cool completely.

Additional Topping Suggestions
> grated parmesan cheese
> thinly sliced tomatoes
> chopped fresh herbs like thyme, basil, or oregano
> caramelized onions
> thinly sliced baked potatoes
> pitted chopped olives
> sautéed vegetables, like squash, zucchini, or eggplant

For thousands of years virtually all good paints and varnishes were made with hempseed oil as the drying agent.

Olive Hempnut Bread

MAKES 1 LOAF

2 tablespoons hempseed oil
1 teaspoon crushed red pepper flakes
2 teaspoons fresh thyme, chopped
1 2-ounce package dry active yeast
1/3 cup warm water
2 1/2–3 cups unbleached white or bread flour
2 tablespoons sugar
1 teaspoon salt
2 large eggs, lightly beaten
1 cup kalamata olives, pitted
1/3 cup hempnuts, toasted
1 egg yolk, beaten

Combine the hempseed oil and red pepper flakes in a small skillet. Place over medium heat and cook just until pepper is fragrant (about 1 minute). Remove from the heat and stir in the chopped thyme. Set aside to cool.

Combine the yeast and warm water in a small bowl. Allow to sit for 5 minutes, or until creamy. Combine the flour, sugar, and salt in a large bowl and make a well in the center. Combine the beaten eggs, yeast mixture, and spiced oil mixture and pour it into the well. Incorporate the flour gradually with your fingers or a wooden spoon until the dough is cohesive enough to be turned out onto a lightly-floured surface.

Knead the dough by hand until smooth and elastic (about 8 minutes). Place in an oiled bowl and cover with plastic wrap. Allow to rise at room temperature for 1 1/2 hours.

Punch down the dough and place on a lightly-floured surface. Gently roll the dough into a 14-inch square. Allow it to sit for 3 to 4 minutes. Scatter the olives and hempnuts evenly over the surface, pressing lightly into the dough. Roll up the dough like a jelly-roll to enclose the ingredients. Place it seam-side down on a baking sheet. Tuck the open ends under to make it smooth and sealed. Pat the loaf to flatten slightly into an oval about 2-inches thick. Cover with plastic wrap and let rise at room temperature about 30 minutes.

→

Meanwhile, preheat oven to 350°F. Uncover the loaf, brush with beaten egg yolk, and bake for 30 to 35 minutes, or until richly browned and hollow sounding when tapped. Cool on a wire rack. Serve warm or cooled.

Manchego Hemp Tuile

MAKES 6

$^1/4$ cup hempnuts
1 cup manchego cheese, grated

Preheat oven to 350°F. Mix the hempnuts and cheese together in a bowl. Line a baking sheet with wax paper. Place 6 piles of cheese hempnut mix on the sheet in your own desired shapes. Place in the oven and bake for 10 to15 minutes, until melted and starting to brown. Take out and let cool. Serve.

Hemp Maize Bread
with Scallions, Roasted Red Pepper, & Cheddar Cheese

MAKES ONE 9-INCH LOAF (16 SERVINGS)

$1^1/2$ cups unbleached white flour

$3/4$ cup hemp flour

$3/4$ cup cornmeal

$1/4$ cup sugar

1 tablespoon baking powder

$1/2$ teaspoon salt

$1/4$ teaspoon baking soda

8 tablespoons (1 stick) chilled unsalted butter

$1^1/2$ cups buttermilk

3 large eggs

2 ears corn, cooked, kernels removed

$1^1/2$ cups cheddar cheese, shredded

$3/4$ cup green onions, thinly sliced

1 large red pepper, roasted, peeled, and diced

Preheat oven to 400°F. Butter a 9-inch square baking pan and set it aside.

Combine the white and hemp flours, cornmeal, sugar, baking powder, salt, and baking soda in a large bowl. Use a pastry blender or two knives to cut in the butter until the mixture resembles peas in texture.

Beat together the buttermilk and eggs with wire whisk until well blended. Stir in the corn, cheese, green onions, and red pepper. Spread the mixture into the prepared pan.

Bake for 40 to 45 minutes, or until golden and you can insert a toothpick in the center and it comes out clean. Serve.

Whole Wheat Hempnut Cranberry Bread

MAKES 1 LOAF

1 2-ounce package dry active yeast

3/4 cup warm water

1 1/2 cups whole wheat flour

1/4 cup nonfat dry milk powder

1 1/2 teaspoons salt

1 large egg

2 tablespoons hempseed oil

2 tablespoons honey

3/4 cup bread flour

1/2 cup dried cranberries

1/2 cup hempnuts, toasted (plus more for sprinkling)

Egg Wash

1 large egg, lightly beaten

1 tablespoon milk

Preheat oven to 375°F. Grease a 9- x 5-inch loaf pan and set it aside.

Combine the yeast and warm water in a medium bowl. Allow to sit for 5 minutes, or until creamy. Combine the whole wheat flour, nonfat dry milk powder, and salt in a separate large bowl and make a well in the center. Mix together the egg, hempseed oil, and honey and combine with the yeast mixture. Pour the wet ingredients into the well, and mix until a batterlike dough forms. Add the bread flour 1/4 cup at a time to form a shaggy mass of dough that can be lifted and placed on a work surface. Let sit for 3 to 5 minutes to allow the whole wheat flour to fully absorb the moisture of the mixture.

Knead dough by hand for 10 minutes, until soft and elastic. Place in a greased bowl and cover with plastic wrap. Let rise at room temperature for 1 hour, or until doubled in volume.

Punch down the dough. Pat into a circle and sprinkle with cranberries and hempnuts. Knead for a few minutes to incorporate the ingredients, then cover with plastic wrap and allow to sit for 5 to 6 minutes. Flatten the dough into an oval the same length as the loaf pan. Fold the dough lengthwise in half and pinch the seam tightly together. Drop the mass into the prepared pan seam side down. Tuck the ends of the dough under and gently push the dough into the corners of the pan with your fingers. Cover with plastic wrap and let rise at room temperature until level with the edge of the pan (approximately 35 to 45 minutes).

Brush the loaf with the egg wash and sprinkle liberally with the additional hempnuts. Bake in middle of the oven for about 40 minutes, or until it is hard and sounds hollow when tapped on bottom. Remove the finished bread from the pan and allow to cool on a wire rack. Serve.

In the 30's

Henry Ford built and powered a car with Hemp.

In the early 1900s, Henry Ford recognized that 90% of all fossil fuel used in the world today should be replaced with biomass, such as cornstalks, cannabis, waste paper, and the like. Biomass can be converted to methane, methanol, or gasoline at a fraction of the current cost of oil, coal, or nuclear energy. Unlike fossil fuel, biomass comes from living plants that continue to remove carbon dioxide from the atmosphere through photosynthesis. When hemp is grown for biomass, CO_2 is taken in and metabolized by the plants, generating oxygen in the process. When the biomass is burned as fuel, the CO_2 is released back into the air, thereby maintaining a balanced CO_2 cycle. By contrast, burning fossil fuels releases carbon back into the atmosphere with no means of reabsorption.

Chocolate Banana Hempnut Bread

MAKES 1 LOAF

    1 cup mashed ripe bananas (3 medium bananas)
    2 large eggs
    $1/3$ cup vegetable oil
    $1/3$ cup whole milk
    $1^1/2$ cups unbleached white flour
    $1/2$ cup hemp flour
    1 cup sugar
    2 teaspoons baking powder
    $1/4$ teaspoon salt
    1 cup semi-sweet chocolate chips
    $1/4$ cup hempnuts, toasted

Preheat oven to 350°F. Grease and flour a 9- x 5-inch loaf pan.

Beat the bananas, eggs, vegetable oil, and milk with wire whisk until well blended. Stir in the white and hemp flours, sugar, baking powder, and salt until combined. Add the chocolate chips and hempnuts and pour entire mixture into the prepared pan. Bake for 65 minutes, or until you are able to insert a toothpick in the center and it comes out clean. Allow to cool in the pan for 10 minutes. Remove bread from pan to cool on a wire rack.

Hemp Biscuits

MAKES 12–15 BISCUITS

12 tablespoons (1$1/2$ sticks) unsalted butter
3 cups unbleached white flour
1 tablespoon salt
3 tablespoons baking powder
5 tablespoons sugar
$1/2$ cup hempnuts
$1/2$ cup buttermilk
1$1/2$ cups ice water

Preheat oven to 375°F. Cut butter in small pieces and set aside in a small bowl. Mix the dry ingredients in a separate bowl. Add the butter and mix together until butter is incorporated and batter resembles small peas in texture. Add the buttermilk and ice water and mix by hand.

Roll the dough out to $1/2$-inch thick square and cut cookie shapes with circular cutter until all the dough is used up. (Preferable size is 1$1/2$ inches in diameter.)

Bake for 15 minutes.

Note: Do not overmix. Knead only until the dough comes together, then stop.

Hempnut Sage Buttermilk Biscuits

MAKES 8 BISCUITS

$2^1/2$ cups cake flour
1 tablespoon baking powder
1 tablespoon sugar
$^1/2$ teaspoon salt
8 tablespoons (1 stick) cold unsalted butter, cut into pieces
$^1/3$ cup hempnuts, toasted (plus more for sprinkling)
2 tablespoons fresh sage, chopped
1 cup buttermilk (plus more for glazing)
8 whole fresh sage leaves for garnish

Preheat oven to 475°F. Combine the flour, baking powder, sugar, and salt in a large bowl. Cut in the butter with a pastry blender or knives until the mixture resembles a coarse meal in texture. Stir in the hempnuts and sage. Gradually add buttermilk until the flour mixture is moist.

Remove the dough to a lightly-floured work surface and pat it out to a $1^1/2$-inch thickness. Use a lightly-floured $2^1/2$-inch round biscuit cutter to cut the dough into individual biscuits. Gather up the scraps, pat them together, and cut again until no dough remains. Place the biscuits on a greased baking sheet.

Lightly brush the tops of biscuits with buttermilk. Place a sage leaf in the center of each biscuit and sprinkle lightly with toasted hempnuts. Bake 15 minutes, or until golden brown. Remove to a wire rack to cool. Serve warm.

Hempnut Cranberry-Quinoa Muffins

MAKES 10 MUFFINS

1/2 cup uncooked quinoa
1 cup water
3/4 cup unbleached white flour
1/4 cup hemp flour
1 cup quinoa flour
1/4 teaspoon salt
1 teaspoon baking soda
1/2 cup light brown sugar, packed
1 egg
4 tablespoons (1/2 stick) unsalted butter, melted
1 1/4 cups plain yogurt
1 teaspoon vanilla extract
1/2 cup dried cranberries

Preheat oven to 375°F. Oil muffin pans. Rinse the quinoa and bring to a boil with 1 cup water in a small saucepan. Cover, reduce to a simmer, and continue to simmer until the water is absorbed (about 15 minutes). Drain the quinoa and set aside.

In the meantime, combine the three flours, salt, baking soda, and brown sugar in a mixing bowl. Beat the egg, butter, yogurt, and vanilla together, then add the dried cranberries. Stir the wet ingredients into the dry. Add the quinoa and mix with a spatula, scraping up from the bottom so that the flour is mixed in thoroughly. Scoop the batter into the muffin cups and bake for 25 to 30 minutes, until firm and light brown on top. Serve.

Variation: Make plain Hempnut Quinoa Muffins without the cranberries.

Hempnut Cookies

MAKES 4 DOZEN

16 tablespoons (2 sticks) unsalted butter, softened
1 cup sugar
1 cup light brown sugar, packed
2 whole eggs
1 teaspoon vanilla extract
2$\frac{1}{2}$ cups oatmeal flour
2 cups unbleached white flour
$\frac{1}{4}$ teaspoon salt
1 teaspoon baking powder
1 teaspoon baking soda
1$\frac{1}{2}$ cups hempnuts

Preheat the oven to 375°F. Mix the softened butter, sugar, brown sugar, eggs, and vanilla until creamy. In a separate bowl, mix the oatmeal and white flours, salt, baking powder, baking soda, and hempnuts.

Mix dry ingredients slowly into wet ingredients, stirring until smooth.

Make golf ball-sized balls of dough and place onto a baking sheet, leaving room between each for expansion during baking. Bake for 6 minutes.

Allow the cookies to cool on the baking sheet for 2 minutes before transferring them to a wire rack to cool. Store in airtight containers.

Shichimi Togarashi is a staple seasoning widely used in Japan that features toasted hempseed.

Lemon Hemparoons

Makes 3 dozen

> 1 14-ounce bag sweetened flaked coconut (about 4 cups lightly packed)
> 2/3 cup hempnuts, toasted
> 1/2 cup (plus 2 tablespoons) finely ground almonds
> 1 tablespoon lemon peel, grated
> 1 14-ounce can sweetened condensed milk
> 1 tablespoon pure vanilla extract

Preheat oven to 325°F. Generously grease a baking sheet and set it aside. Mix together the coconut, hempnuts, almonds, and lemon peel until well combined. Stir in the condensed milk and vanilla with a wooden spoon.

Heap tablespoonfuls of batter onto the prepared baking sheet about one inch apart, pressing to form a slightly mounded shape.

Bake the Hemparoons in the preheated oven for 15 to 17 minutes, or until golden brown. Use a spatula to transfer them to a wire rack to cool. The Hemparoons will harden as they cool. Store in airtight containers.

Toasted Hempnut Oatmeal-Currant Cookies

MAKES 5 DOZEN

1 1/2 cups unbleached white flour
1/2 cup hemp flour
1 teaspoon baking soda
3/4 teaspoon salt
1/2 teaspoon ground cinnamon
1 3/4 cups (3 1/2 sticks) unsalted butter, softened
1 1/4 cups light brown sugar, firmly packed
1 cup sugar
3 large eggs
1/4 cup water
2 teaspoons pure vanilla extract
5 cups rolled oats
1 1/2 cups currants
1/2 cup sweetened flaked coconut, lightly packed
1/2 cup hempnuts, toasted (plus extra for sprinkling)

Preheat oven to 350°F. Sift together the white and hemp flours, baking soda, salt, and cinnamon into a medium bowl and set aside.

Use an electric mixer set on high to beat together the butter, brown sugar, and sugar until light and airy (about 3 to 4 minutes). Add the eggs, water, and vanilla extract and beat all ingredients until smooth. Turn the mixer to a low speed and add the flour mixture until combined and a dough forms. Stir in oats, currants, coconut, and hempnuts. If dough is too soft, refrigerate until firm before shaping and baking cookies.

Heap tablespoonfuls of dough onto ungreased baking sheets about 2 inches apart. Flatten the cookies slightly and sprinkle with 1/2 teaspoon of additional toasted hempnuts.

Bake for 15 minutes in the preheated oven, turning the pan once midway through baking. Allow the cookies to cool on the baking sheet for 2 minutes before transferring them to a wire rack to cool. Store in airtight containers.

Hemp Brownies

MAKES 16 BROWNIES

> 8 tablespoons (1 stick) unsalted butter
> $1/8$ cup unsweetened chocolate
> $1^1/2$ cups sugar
> 2 large eggs
> 1 teaspoon pure vanilla extract
> $3/4$ cup unbleached white flour
> $1/4$ cup hemp flour
> $1/4$ teaspoon salt
> $1/2$ cup toasted hempnuts

Preheat oven to 350°F. Line an 8-inch square pan with aluminum foil. Grease the foil and set the pan aside. In the microwave on a high setting, melt the butter and chocolate in a large bowl for 45 seconds, stir, and microwave for 45 seconds more. Stir until all chocolate is melted and the mixture is smooth.

Stir in the sugar, eggs, and vanilla extract until well blended. Stir in the white and hemp flours and salt until just blended. Stir in the hempnuts, then spread the mixture into the prepared pan.

Bake for 30 to 35 minutes, until you can insert a toothpick in the center and it comes out with fudgey crumbs. Do not overbake. Allow to cool on a wire rack. Use the edges of the foil as handles to lift the brownies out onto a cutting board. Remove the foil and cut brownies into squares. Serve.

Hemp-Crusted Apple Pie

SERVES 6

Apple Filling

    1 tablespoon unsalted butter
    $1/4$ cup light brown sugar
    1 teaspoon cinnamon
    6 Granny Smith apples, peeled, cored, and cut into chunks
    1 cup corn syrup

Melt the butter with the brown sugar and cinnamon in a saucepot. Add the apples and corn syrup. Cook on low heat for 15 minutes, or until all the apples are soft but still intact. Let cool.

Hemp Dough Crust

    $1/2$ tablespoon active dry yeast
    $1/8$ cup warm water
    2 cups cake flour
    $1/4$ pound hemp flour
    1 tablespoon salt
    $1/2$ cup granulated sugar
    $3/8$ cup coarse ground hempseed
    1 teaspoon vanilla extract
    $1/2$–1 cup warm water
    $1 1/2$ cups unsalted butter

Mix the yeast with the warm water and allow to foam for 10 minutes. Combine all the ingredients except for the butter in a stainless steel mixing bowl. Add enough water to form a workable dough. Cover with plastic wrap and allow it to sit for 2 hours. Roll out the dough to a $1/2$-inch thick rectangle.

    Cut the butter into small cubes and allow to soften. Arrange the cubes in the center of the rectangle. Fold both sides of the dough to the center so that they overlap. Roll the dough out again to a $1/2$-inch thick rectangle. Repeat the buttering, folding, and rolling out process 2 more times. After the last fold, cover and place the dough in the refrigerator for 1 to 2 hours.

$\rightarrow$

Take the dough out, cut into 6 even pieces, and roll each piece out as thin as possible.

Preheat oven to 375°F. Grease the sides of 6 muffin tins. Using a 6-inch cookie cutter or a saucer, cut 6 rounds from the dough. Form the crusts into the muffin tins. Fill each tin with the apple filling. Cut the rest of the dough to create the top crusts, pinching dough together at the sides. Bake in the oven for 15 minutes, or until golden brown.

Serve topped with Hemp Ice Cream (page 6).

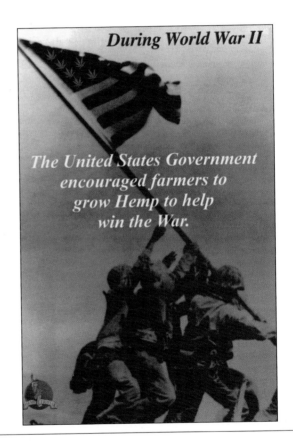

During World War II

The United States Government encouraged farmers to grow Hemp to help win the War.

 Little did George H. W. Bush know when he bailed out of his burning airplane in WWII that 100% of his life-saving parachute webbing was made from American-grown cannabis hemp.

Walnut-Ginger Hemp Tart

MAKES ONE TART

Tart Crust

       1^1/4 cups all-purpose flour

       ^{1}/2 teaspoon salt

       ^{1}/2 teaspoon sugar

       8 tablespoons (1 stick) unsalted butter, chilled

       2 tablespoons ice water

Using a food processor fitted with metal blade, combine the flour, salt, and sugar, pulsing several times. Add the butter and pulse 8–10 seconds until the mixture resembles a coarse meal in texture.

    With the machine running, slowly add the ice water in a steady stream through the feed tube until the dough holds together when pinched without being too wet or sticky. Wrap the dough in plastic and flatten into a disk. Refrigerate for at least 2 hours.

Tart

       1 tart crust disk, chilled

       3 tablespoons hempnuts, toasted

       ^{3}/4 cup walnuts, chopped

       ^{1}/4 cup hempnuts, toasted

       3 large eggs

       1^1/2 cups light brown sugar, firmly packed

       6 tablespoons (^{3}/4 stick) unsalted butter, melted

       2 tablespoons heavy cream

       1 tablespoon ginger root, finely chopped

       1 teaspoon pure vanilla extract

Preheat the oven to 325°F.

    Roll the chilled tart crust onto a lightly-floured surface until it is 12 inches in diameter. Sprinkle the surface with the 3 tablespoons of toasted hempnuts and roll them in gently, until they are pressed into the dough. Turn the crust over so that it is hempnut-side down and place in a 9-inch spring-form tart pan. Form edges by pressing the dough up around the sides of the pan. Remove and discard any excess dough. Fill the tart pan with the walnuts and the ¹/4 cup hempnuts. Refrigerate for 30 minutes.

Beat the eggs, brown sugar, butter, heavy cream, ginger root, and vanilla together with a wire whisk until well blended and smooth. Pour into tart pan covering the nuts. Place the pan on a baking sheet.

Bake in the preheated oven for 55 minutes, until the center is set. Cool on wire rack. Release the edges of the spring-form pan, leaving the tart on the bottom part until it is time to cut and serve. Serve with whipped cream or ice cream.

The Daughters of the American Revolution sewed hemp linens for the Continental Army, without which soldiers may have frozen to death at The Battle of Valley Forge. — *Industrial Hemp,* Hemptech

Blue Agave Nectar Triple Berry Tart
with Rustic Hemp Flour Crust

MAKES 1 TART

Tart Crust (makes 2 disks)

1/4 cup ice water, ice cubes removed

3 tablespoons sour cream

1 cup all-purpose flour

1/4 cup hemp flour

1 teaspoon sugar

1/2 teaspoon salt

7 tablespoons unsalted butter, chilled

Combine the water and sour cream in a small bowl until blended, then set aside. Using a food processor fitted with a metal blade, mix the all-purpose and hemp flours, sugar, and salt, pulsing a few seconds until just combined. Then add the butter and pulse 8 to 10 times until the mixture resembles the texture of a coarse meal.

With the machine running, gradually add the sour cream mixture a tablespoonful at a time until the dough just becomes soft, moist, and will stick together when pinched. Remove the dough from the food processor and divide it in half onto two pieces of plastic wrap. Use the plastic wrap to lift and press the dough into a disk. Wrap tightly and refrigerate at least 2 hours.

Tart Filling

1 tart crust disk, chilled

1/2 cup blueberries

1/2 cup raspberries

1/2 cup strawberries, hulled and sliced

1 tablespoon blue agave nectar (see Glossary)

1 tablespoon unsalted butter, chilled

Egg Wash

1 egg yolk *plus* 1 tablespoon water

1 teaspoon sugar

→

Preheat oven to 400°F. Position a rack in lower third of the oven. On a lightly-floured piece of parchment paper, roll tart crust dough into a circle 11 inches in diameter and 1/8-inch thick. It may be necessary to sprinkle flour over the dough as you roll it out. If the dough becomes too soft, refrigerate it until firm enough to continue rolling. Use a rolling pin to transfer the dough to an ungreased baking sheet.

Spread the berries in the center of the dough, leaving a 2- to 3-inch border. Drizzle agave nectar over fruit and scatter butter pieces across the top. Lift and fold the crust border up over the filling, allowing the dough to overlap and pleat naturally as you go, making a free formed crust. Brush the crust with the egg wash and sprinkle with a teaspoon of sugar.

Bake the tart for 30 to 35 minutes, or until the pastry is golden and crisp. Place baking sheet on wire rack and allow to cool for 10 minutes. Use a wide spatula to gently lift the tart from the baking sheet and finish cooling on a wire rack. Serve warm or at room temperature.

Hempnut Almond Baklava

MAKES 16 PIECES

> 2 cups blanched almonds, chopped
> 2 cups blanched hempnuts
> 1/2 cup sugar
> 1 tablespoon cinnamon
> 10 tablespoons (1 1/4) sticks unsalted butter, melted
> 1 1/2 pounds phyllo dough (see Glossary) in ready-made sheets

Preheat the oven to 250°F. Mix together the almonds, hempnuts, sugar, and cinnamon in a stainless steel bowl. Select a square pan the size of the phyllo sheets. Brush the pan generously with melted butter. Use 4 sheets of phyllo dough for the bottom layer, brushing each one with butter before adding the next one.

Place a fifth sheet of unbuttered phyllo dough over the forth, then sprinkle with the nut-sugar mixture. Continue until all ingredients and all but 5 phyllo sheets are used. 5 sheets need to be reserved for the top layer.

Brush each of the 5 top sheets with ample butter, pouring any remaining butter over the top. Trim edges if necessary. Score the baklava into diamond-shaped pieces being careful not to cut through the bottom layers. Sprinkle water over the baklava. Bake for 1 hour, or until golden. Remove from the oven and allow to cool.

Syrup

> 4 cups sugar
> 3 cups water
> 1/2 cup honey
> 1 piece cinnamon stick
> 5–6 cloves

Put sugar and water into large pot and boil for 5 minutes. Add honey, cinnamon, and cloves. Boil for 5 more minutes. Pour hot syrup over the baklava once it has cooled. Then cut along the scores and through bottom layers and serve.

Hempnut Chocolatissimo

SERVES 6

    1 cup unsalted butter, softened to room temperature
    10 ounces (1¹/4 cups) semi-sweet chocolate
    8 eggs, separated
    1 cup sugar
    1 tablespoon bread crumbs
    ¹/4 cup hempnuts
    1 tablespoon Grand Marnier

Preheat oven to 350°F.

Heat the butter in a pan, then melt the chocolate in the butter. Remove from heat and cool. Beat the 8 egg yolks together with the sugar until fluffy and lemon colored. Add the cooled chocolate mixture. Add the bread crumbs, hempnuts, and the Grand Marnier. Beat the egg whites until stiff, and fold into the chocolate mixture. Butter a sheet pan and pour in the mixture. Bake for 30 minutes in the preheated oven, checking to see if it has risen a little. (It should be slightly spongy to the touch. Be careful not to cook it too long or it will get hard.)

Remove from the oven and allow to cool. The Hempnut Chocolatissimo can be frozen and taken out 30 minutes before serving. It is easier to work with when it is cold. You can cut it and make a layered cake by spreading strawberry or apricot jam between each layer. Serve with some whipped cream and or ice cream.

(The same recipe, unbaked, can be used as a frosting.)

Hempnut Chocolate Truffles

MAKES 2 DOZEN

> 4 ounces bittersweet chocolate
> 3/8 cup heavy cream
> 2 tablespoons unsalted butter
> 2 tablespoons brandy or other aromatic liquor
> 3/8 cup hempnuts, toasted

Use a sharp knife to cut the chocolate into chunks. Place in a metal bowl and add the butter and cream. Wrap the bowl tightly with plastic wrap. Place the chocolate mixture in a double boiler (see Glossary) and allow the mixture to melt for 5 minutes.

Stir the mixture until smooth, then add the brandy. Refrigerate for 2 hours until it sets. Use a spoon to shape the chocolate into balls. Roll the balls in toasted hempnuts until coated on all sides. Serve

Carrot-Orange Hempnut Cake
with Cream Cheese Frosting

MAKES 1 CAKE

Cream Cheese Frosting

> 1 8-ounce package cream cheese, softened
> 8 tablespoons (1 stick) unsalted butter, softened
> 2 tablespoons fresh-squeezed orange juice
> 2 teaspoons orange peel, grated
> 1 pound box confectioners' sugar

Beat the cream cheese and butter until well blended and smooth. Add the orange juice and orange peel, beating until well combined. Add the confectioners' sugar and beat until smooth. Refrigerate until thick enough to spread (about 30 minutes).

Carrot-Orange Cake

 1 1/2 cups vegetable oil
 1 cup light brown sugar, firmly packed
 1 cup sugar
 4 large eggs
 1/3 cup fresh-squeezed orange juice
 1 tablespoon orange peel, grated
 1 3/4 cup unbleached white flour
 1/2 cup hemp flour
 2 teaspoons baking soda
 1 teaspoon baking powder
 1/2 teaspoon salt
 1 teaspoon ground cinnamon
 1 teaspoon ground ginger
 1/2 teaspoon ground nutmeg
 3 cups carrots, peeled and finely grated
 1 cup hempnuts, toasted
 1 cup raisins or currants

Preheat the oven to 325°F. Butter and flour two 9-inch round cake pans and set them aside. Using an electric mixer set on medium high, beat together the vegetable oil and brown and white sugars until well blended. Add the eggs one at a time until blended. Beat in the orange juice and orange peel.

In a separate bowl, sift together the white and hemp flours, baking soda, baking powder, salt, and spices. Add the flour mix to the egg mixture and stir until blended. Stir in the carrots, 1/2 cup of the hempnuts, and raisins.

Distribute the batter equally into the prepared pans and bake on the center rack for 50 minutes, or until you can insert a toothpick in the center and it comes out clean. Allow the cakes to cool in the pan for 15 minutes. Remove the cakes from the pan and continue to cool completely on a wire rack.

To finish the cake, spread 1 cup of Cream Cheese Frosting over the top of one of the cakes. Place the other half directly on top of the frosting-covered cake to create a two-layered cake. Continue to frost the sides and top of the cake with remaining frosting. Garnish the sides with remaining 1/2 cup toasted hempnuts. Refrigerate until ready to serve.

Virgo's Vegan Carrot Cake
with Hempnut Whipped Cream

SERVES 6

Cake Crust

> 2 cups almonds
>
> 2 cups dates

Chop the dates and almonds into small pieces. Knead, and form into a 9-inch pie mold. Place in the freezer.

Cake Filling

> 2 cups dates, soaked
>
> 2 pounds carrots, juiced, to yield 2 cups carrot pulp
>
> 1 1/2 cups carrot juice
>
> 2 cups raw coconut meat, minced
>
> 1/4 cup ginger, minced
>
> 3/4 cup golden raisins, soaked, then minced
>
> 2 cups raw walnuts, chopped into small pieces
>
> 1 1/2 teaspoons ground cinnamon
>
> 1/2 teaspoon cardamom
>
> 1 teaspoon nutmeg

Mix all the filling ingredients in a food processor until blended. Pour and form the mixture into the chilled piecrust.

Hempnut Whipped Cream

> 1 1/2 cups hempnuts, soaked in water for 2 hours
>
> 1/2 cup fresh-squeezed orange juice

Drain the hempnuts and grind them in a food processor. Add the orange juice and blend until smooth and airy. If too stiff, add a little water.

To serve, spread the Hempnut Whipped Cream on top of the Vegan Carrot Cake. Serve on dessert plates.

Viennese Hemp Cake
with Chocolate-Raisin Sauce

Serves 12

8 tablespoons (1 stick) unsalted butter

6 eggs, separated

7 tablespoons semi-sweet chocolate, softened

3 tablespoons confectioners' sugar

3 tablespoons sugar

3 tablespoons ground walnuts

3 tablespoons hempnuts

7 tablespoons bread crumbs

3 tablespoons unbleached white flour

extra butter and confectioners' sugar for the tin cans

Preheat the oven to 350°F. Butter and sugar 12 sweet condensed milk cans or other small tin cans.

Place the butter, egg yolks, chocolate, and sugars together in a bowl and whisk until fluffy. Beat the egg whites until firm and fold into the chocolate mixture. Slowly mix in the walnuts, hempnuts, bread crumbs, and white flour.

Fill the tin cans 3/4 full with the mixture. Place in a boiling bain-marie (see Glossary). Cover them 3/4 of the way with tin foil and bake for 30 to 40 minutes, or until firm. Allow to cool.

Chocolate-Raisin Sauce

1 cup sugar

1 cup heavy cream

8 ounces (1 cup) semi-sweet chocolate

1/4 cup walnuts

1/4 cup raisins

1 teaspoon Grand Marnier

1/4 cup hempnuts, toasted

→

Mix together the sugar and heavy cream in a saucepan on medium heat. Add chunks of chocolate little by little until the chocolate melts. Mix in the nuts, raisins, and Grand Marnier.

Dip each cake in Chocolate-Raisin Sauce, roll them in hempnuts, and serve with whipped cream and or ice cream.

Hemp Pound Cake

MAKES 1 CAKE

> 1 1/4 cups cake flour
> 1/2 cup hemp flour
> 1/4 teaspoon salt
> 1 cup sugar
> 12 tablespoons (1 1/2 sticks) unsalted butter, softened
> 3 large eggs
> 1 teaspoon pure vanilla extract

Preheat oven to 325°F. Butter and flour a 9- x 5-inch loaf pan and set aside. Sift together the cake and hemp flours and salt in a medium bowl and set aside.

Using an electric mixer on high, beat together the sugar and butter until light and airy (about 4 minutes) in a large bowl. Add the eggs, one at a time, beating after each addition until combined. Stir in the vanilla extract. Turn the mixer on low speed and gradually add the flour mixture, beating until just combined. Spoon the batter into the prepared pan.

Bake the pound cake for 1 hour in the preheated oven, or until lightly golden and you can insert a toothpick in the center and it comes out clean. Remove and allow to cool in the pan for 10 minutes. Remove from the pan to a wire rack to cool completely. Serve.

Steamed Hempnut Banana Cake

SERVES 6

> 2 tablespoons unsalted butter, softened
> 2 1/2 cups unbleached white flour
> 1 tablespoon baking powder
> 1 1/2 teaspoons ground cinnamon
> 1 teaspoon baking soda
> 1/4 teaspoon salt
> 3 large eggs (room temperature)
> 1 teaspoon fresh-squeezed lemon juice
> 1 cup brown sugar
> 3 ripe bananas, mashed
> 1/2 cup nonfat yogurt
> 2 tablespoons unsalted butter, melted
> 1 tablespoon vanilla extract
> 1/2 cup hempnuts
> 1/2 gallon water for steaming

Generously grease a 10-inch baking tin with the softened butter. Sift together the flour, baking powder, cinnamon, baking soda, and salt.

Break the eggs into a large bowl. Beat vigorously until tripled in volume. Add the lemon juice and brown sugar and beat for 3 minutes. Add the mashed bananas, yogurt, melted butter, vanilla extract, and hempnuts, beating well after each addition. Fold in the flour mixture. Pour the batter into the greased tin.

Bring the water to boil in a large pot. Place the cake tin in a bain-marie (see Glossary) over the boiling water. Cover and steam over high heat for 50 minutes, or until the cake springs to the touch.

To serve, remove the Steamed Hempnut Banana Cake from the tin and place onto a plate. Cut into slices. Serve warm or cooled.

Hemp Milk Eggless Custard

Yields 6 4-ounce ramekins

Caramel

> 1/2 cup sugar
> 1/4 cup water
> juice of half a lemon

Mix the sugar, water, and lemon juice in a saucepan. Heat over a medium-high flame. Brush the sides of the pan with a pastry brush making sure there is not any granules of sugar clinging to the sides of the pan. Allow the mixture to boil. Once the mixture is a light caramel color, remove from flame. The caramel will continue to darken. Pour and swirl the caramel in each ramekin just enough to coat so that caramel clings to all sides. Set aside.

Custard

> 1 cup light cream
> 4 tablespoons condensed milk
> 1 teaspoon cinnamon
> 1/2 teaspoon ground ginger
> 12 mint leaves
> 4 gelatin leaves
> 1 recipe Hemp Milk (page 4)

Combine the light cream, condensed milk, cinnamon, ginger, and mint leaves in a saucepan and bring to a simmer. Soak the gelatin in cold water until soft (about 5 minutes). Add the gelatin to the warm mixture and stir. Add the Hemp Milk and taste for sweetness. Add more condensed milk or honey if desired.

Pour the custard into the caramel-lined ramekins. Wrap with plastic wrap and refrigerate for a minimum of 5 hours.

To serve, use a paring knife to run the blade alongside the ramekin, loosening the caramel from the sides. Turn the Hemp Milk Eggless Custard over onto a plate.

Pumpkin Cheesecake
with Gingersnap & Pecan Crust

YIELDS ONE 9-INCH CAKE

Gingersnap & Pecan Crust

    17 gingersnap cookies, broken into fourths

    2 tablespoons pecans, toasted

    1 tablespoon sugar

    2 pinches salt

    $1/4$ cup unsalted butter

    $1/2$ teaspoon ground cinnamon

    $1/2$ teaspoon ground cardamom

    $1/2$ teaspoon ground ginger

Preheat oven to 350°F. Grease the sides of a 9- x 9- x $1/2$-inch spring-form pan.

    Blend the gingersnap cookies, pecans, sugar, salt, butter, and spices in a food processor until ground to a medium consistency. Use your fingers or the back of a spoon to press the mixture into the prepared pan. Press down thoroughly until the crumbs are evenly distributed.

Pumpkin Cheesecake Filling

    1 cup pumpkin puree

    1 cup sugar

    2 cups heavy cream

    1 24-ounce package cream cheese, softened to room temperature

    2 large eggs

    2 large yolks

Combine the pumpkin puree and sugar in a saucepan and heat to a sputtering simmer, stirring constantly for 5 minutes. Turn the heat to low and cook for an additional 3 to 5 minutes, until thick and dark. Place the mixture in a food processor and process for 1 minute, leaving the vent open to release steam. Incorporate the heavy cream and cream cheese, blend for 30 seconds, and then add the eggs and egg yolks. Blend for 10 seconds until mixed. Pour the filling into the spring-form pan to cover the crust.

$\rightarrow$

Bake in a bain-marie (see Glossary) at 350°F for 1 hour and 15 minutes. Allow to cool at room temperature for 1 hour. Chill for at least 5 hours. Serve with whole pecans and whipped cream.

Key Lime Pie

SERVES 6

    1 1/3 cups graham cracker crumbs
    1/3 cup confectioners' sugar
    1/3 cup hempnuts
    6 tablespoons (3/4 stick) unsalted butter, melted, then allowed to
        cool
    4 egg yolks
    1 3/4 cups condensed milk
    1/2 cup key lime juice, or fresh-squeezed lime juice as a substitute
    1/2 tablespoon cream of tartar

Preheat the oven to 350°F. Combine the graham crackers crumbs, sugar, hemp-nuts, and butter in a bowl. Press the mixture into a pie plate to form a crust and bake in the preheated oven for 10 minutes, until lightly brown, and allow to cool.

Beat the egg yolks until light in color. Stir in the condensed milk, lime juice, and cream of tartar. Add more lime juice to taste if desired. Pour the mixture into the pie crust. Bake for an additional 10 minutes, or until firm. Refrigerate and serve.

"Aire" Hemp Bread Pudding

with Jamaican Rum Hard Sauce

Serves 10–12

Jamaican Rum Hard Sauce

> 1 cup confectioners' sugar
> 5 tablespoons unsalted butter, softened
> 2 tablespoons dark rum
> 1/2 teaspoon pure vanilla extract

Using an electric mixer set on high speed, beat together the confectioners' sugar and butter until smooth and creamy (about 3 minutes). Add the rum and vanilla and beat until smooth. Cover and refrigerate until ready to serve.

"Aire" Hemp Bread Pudding

> 1 recipe Hemp Pound Cake (page 264), cut into 1/2-inch slices
> 4 large egg yolks
> 3 large eggs
> 1/2 cup sugar
> 1 3/4 cups milk
> 1 1/4 cups heavy cream
> 1 teaspoon ground allspice
> 1 cup pineapple, cut into 1/2-inch cubes
> 1 cup mango, cut into 1/2-inch cubes
> 1/2 cup sweetened flaked coconut, lightly packed

Preheat oven to 325°F. Butter a 13- x 9-inch glass baking dish and set it aside.

Place slices of Hemp Pound Cake on a baking sheet in the oven for 15 to 20 minutes, until they begin to dry out and toast. Remove and cool on a wire rack. Whisk together the egg yolks, eggs, and sugar in a large bowl and set aside. Combine the milk, heavy cream, and allspice in a heavy-bottom saucepan over medium-high heat. Cook until bubbles begin to form around edges, but do not allow it to boil. Slowly pour the hot milk mixture into the egg mixture, whisking continuously. Pass the pudding mixture through a strainer into a clean bowl.

Place half the cake slices on bottom of a prepared dish. Sprinkle evenly with half the pineapple, mango, and coconut flakes. Repeat with the remaining cake slices and remaining fruit and coconut flakes. Pour the pudding mixture over the cake slices. Press down with a spatula to moisten the cake thoroughly. Place the dish in a larger roasting pan. Pour hot water into the roasting pan so that it comes halfway up the sides of the pudding dish.

Bake the bread pudding in the preheated oven for 55 to 60 minutes, until you can insert a toothpick in the center and it comes out clean. Remove from the oven, then carefully remove from the roasting pan.

Cut the "Aire" Hemp Bread Pudding into squares and serve warm or cold with spoonfuls of Jamaican Rum Hard Sauce.

The Monkey Bar

SERVES 6

$^1/4$ cup unsalted butter
8 ounces (1 cup) semi-sweet chocolate
1 tablespoon Grand Marnier
1 cup sugar
6 bananas
$^1/2$ cup hempnuts

Melt the butter with the chocolate in a saucepot. Remove from the heat and add the Grand Marnier and the sugar. Peel the bananas and dip each one in the warm chocolate. Coat the chocolate covered bananas with hempnuts. Serve with ice cream or whipped cream.

Beggar's Purse
with Strawberry Compote & Chocolate Sauce

SERVES 6

Chocolate Ganache

$1/2$ pound semi-sweet chocolate

1 cup heavy cream

2 tablespoons Grand Marnier

Place the chocolate and the heavy cream in a stainless steel bowl. Cover with plastic wrap. Put a pot of water to boil. Reduce to a simmer and place the stainless steel bowl over the simmering water. Keep over the hot water for 15 minutes, or until the chocolate has melted completely. Remove from the heat and add the Grand Marnier. Mix thoroughly. Place in refrigerator until completely cold and firm. Set aside.

Strawberry Compote

2 cups fresh strawberries, sliced

1 cup raw cane sugar

2 tablespoons fresh-squeezed lemon juice

Mix the strawberries, sugar, and lemon juice in a pot and simmer for 30 minutes, or until thick and pulpy. Set aside to cool.

Chocolate Sauce

$1/2$ cup heavy cream

1 tablespoon honey

1 tablespoon vanilla extract, or to taste

$1/2$ cup melted chocolate

Combine the heavy cream and honey in a pot and bring to a boil. Remove from heat. Add the vanilla extract and melted chocolate. Mix thoroughly.

Beggar's Purse

    6 fresh wonton wrappers
    1 cup hempnuts
2¼ cups Chocolate Ganache
    1 recipe Strawberry Compote
      Chocolate Sauce
      coconut oil or other high-temperature frying oil
    1 pint vanilla ice cream

Place the wonton wrappers on a working surface. Slice a half-inch off the side of each one and place aside to be used to tie the purse. Lay out each wrapper and sprinkle with enough hempnuts to cover the surface. Using a rolling pin, roll the hempnuts into the wonton wrappers.

Place 3 tablespoons of Chocolate Ganache in the center of each wonton wrapper. Position 2 tablespoons of Strawberry Compote on top of the ganache. Pull the four corners of the wrapper up to the center to create a pouch. Pinch the wrapper together just under the top of the pouch, like holding the mouth of an inflated balloon. Tie off with the reserved strand of wonton wrapper. Place in the freezer so that they do not lose their form.

Heat the oil in a pot deep enough to cover the purses. When the oil reaches 350°F, put each purse in the oil and fry until golden brown. Place on paper towels to absorb excess oil.

To serve, arrange each Beggar's Purse on a plate next to a dollop of Strawberry Compote and a ball of ice cream. Drizzle the Chocolate Sauce over the top.

Bibliography

Bocsa, Ivan, and Karus, Michael. *The Cultivation of Hemp: Botany, Varieties, Cultivation, and Harvesting*. Hemptech, 1998.

Brown, L. of Worldwatch Institute,. 1974 estimates, adjusted using 1988 figures from USDA Agricultural Statistics, 1989. Tables 74, High protein feeds, and 75, Feed concentrates fed to livestock & poultry; B. Resenberg, "Curb on US Waste Urged to Help the World's Hungry," New York Times (October 25, 1974): EarthSave, Realities for the 90s (Santa Cruz, CA: 1991).

Conrad, Chris. *Hemp for Health*. Healing Arts Press, 1997.

Conrad, Chris. *Lifeline to the Future*. Creative Xpressions Publications, 1994.

Jones, Kenneth. *Nutritional and Medicinal Guide to Hemp Seed*. Rainforest Botanical Lab, 1995.

Leson, Gero; Pless, Petra; and Roulac, John. *Hemp Foods and Oil for Health*. Hemptech, 1999.

Molleken, H. "Trans-Fatty Acids in Heated Hempseed Oil." *The Journal of the International Hemp Association*, 1998.

Molotosky, I. "Animal Antibiotics Tied to Illness in Humans." *New York Times*, Feb. 22, 1987.

Nova Institute, Ed. *Hanfsamen und Hanfol als Lebens—und Heilmittel*. Germany: Verlag die Werktatt, 1998.

Pimentel, D. and Pimentel, M. *Food, Energy and Society*. University Press of Colorado, 1996.

Glossary

Abuelita Chocolate: Mexican bitter chocolate used for making mole sauce, hot chocolate, and other Mexican treats. Found at any local Mexican market.

Aioli: Mayonnaise made with garlic.

Amish Grain Mill: An apparatus used to finely grind grains, beans, nuts, and seeds. Made entirely of wood, it is also a manually operated machine as the Amish do not use electricity.

Agave Nectar: A naturally sweet syrup made from the agave cactus, it's also used to produce tequila.

Appetizer: Light food served as a starting plate before the main meal.

Asafetida Powder: A flavoring obtained from a large fennel-like plant native to Iran and India. It is used in many Indian dishes and can be found in a powdered form at most Indian markets. Its taste is quite garlicky and it should be used in small amounts.

Baby Bok Choy: A leaf-headed Chinese vegetable found at specialty produce markets or any local Asian market.

Bain-Marie: A water bath used to cook food slowly in a cooking vessel surrounded by hot water.

Baste: The process of wetting foods with sauces or other liquids while cooking. This gives the food a nice glaze and prevents it from drying out.

Batter: A mixture of flour, egg, and other ingredients, used in recipes for pancakes,

cakes, breads, and crêpes. Batters are usually semi-thick, although they can vary in thickness.

Beurre Noisette: A French term for "hazelnut butter," or brown butter, referring to its color as the butter is heated until browned.

Bias: A term for cutting something at a 45-degree angle.

Blanche: Referring to almonds, hempnuts, or other nuts: Put a pot of water to boil. Add the nuts and cook for 30 seconds. Drain the water and use the nuts.

Boil: To cook something in a water temperature of 212°F (100°C) or higher.

Caramelization: The process of browning sugar in a pan over high heat. The caramelization temperature of sugar is approximately 320°–360°F (160°–182°C).

Carrot Pulp: Carrot pulp is what that remains after juicing a carrot. If using a champion juicer, the pulp comes out of the front spout.

Champion Juicer: A motor-powered juicing device with multiple attachments. It has two separate exits: one for juice and the other for pulp, seeds, etc. A grain mill attachment is also available.

Chiffonade: Leafy vegetables or herbs sliced into fine shreds.

Chop: A term for cutting something into pieces of the same size.

Clarified Butter: Butter cooked until its cream and water separate. Removing the water leaves pure butter fat, giving it a higher burning point.

Colander: A perforated bowl, with or without a base or legs, used to strain foods.

Composites: Industrial products, such as particle board, made up of different elements, such as binders or the woody fibers from trees or hemp.

Concassee: Tomatoes that have been peeled, seeded, and chopped.

Couscous: Pellets of semolina, usually cooked by steaming.

Crêpe: A thin pancake made with egg, flour, and water.

Curry: A mixture of spices primarily used in Indian cuisine. These spices include cardamom, cloves, cinnamon, chilies, fenugreek, fennel, ginger, allspice, garlic, and others.

Dice: To cut into small cubes (smaller than a chop).

Double Boiler: A pot of boiling water with a second pot that fits on top of the first. It is used to melt chocolate, make delicate egg sauces (béarnaise, hollandaise, etc.), and for other applications that require indirect heat.

Dry Sauté: To sauté something without fat using an iron skillet or non-stick pan.

Edamame Beans: Soybean pods.

Egg Wash: The combination of beaten eggs with a little water used to paint pastries and breads, or to seal raviolis, dumplings, or egg rolls. When something is washed with egg wash and then baked, it produces a beautiful golden color as well as sealing it.

Emulsion: A mixture of a few liquids, one being oil-based and another water-based, in which tiny globules of one are suspended within the other. This is usually made possible by stabilizers such as egg or mustard.

Essential Fatty Acids: Named the "good" or polyunsaturated fats, they are found in some plants, fish, and nuts. Linoleic acid and alpha-linolenic acid are the two fatty acids that are essential to our diet in order to maintain normal body functions such as heart action and tissue integrity. EFAs account for more than 75 percent of the fatty acids found in hempseed oil.

Fat: One of the basic nutrients used by the body for energy. "Fat is flavor."

Five Spice: A Chinese blend of spices consisting of cinnamon, coriander seeds, star anise, cloves, and pepper.

Flat-Top: A thick plate of cast iron or steel that is placed over the fire to diffuse heat, dispersing it more evenly than would an open burner.

Flour: The material ground from seedmeal or seedcake; also the residue of hempseed after crushing. Varying with hulling and crushing techniques, flour contains protein, hulls, and residual oil and is used for baking, brewing, and animal food.

Food Mill: A type of strainer with a crank arm that is operated by a curved blade pushing the food through the strainer. It is used to puree soft foods.

Food Processor: A machine with changeable blades and disks. It is used to puree, chop, dice, grind, knead, slice, shred, julienne, and emulsify foods.

Free-Range: A term that refers to animals that are raised in an unconfined area.

Fritter: Different foods that are mixed into a batter and deep-fried and usually served with a sauce and salad.

Ganache: A filling or glaze made from chocolate, cream, and/or other ingredients.

Garam Masala: An Indian mixture of spices available in any number of varieties, most of which contain cinnamon, bay leaves, cumin seeds, coriander seeds, cardamom seeds, black pepper corns, dried chilies, cloves, and nutmeg.

Garnish: An edible decoration or accompaniment to a dish.

Ghee: Butter that has been slowly melted and heated until the milk fat solids separate from the golden liquid on the surface. Also called clarified butter. The only difference is that the process is taken a step further. It is then heated on a low flame until the milk solid turns brown, giving the butter a nutty, caramel flavor as well as a higher smoking point. It can be purchased at most Middle Eastern and Indian markets, although it can easily be made at home.

Green Birds Eye Chili: Only about 1 to $1^1/2$ inches long, this chili packs a fiery punch that doesn't dissipate after cooking. The thin-fleshed chili ranges in color from green to red when fully ripe. When dry, the chili forms a hook in the shape of a bird's beak.

Grill: A term for cooking food on top of a radiant heat source.

Guajillo Peppers: A mild to spicy Mexican pepper that can be found dried at any local Mexican market.

Haricot Vert: French green beans that are about 4 to 6 inches long and very thin. They can be found at any local specialty produce market.

Hempseed: The seeds of the hemp plant that contain 25 percent protein and whose oil content is between 25–30 percent. This oil can be extracted to produce a nutritious and superior quality oil.

Hempseed Meal: The portion of the seed that remains after the oil has been pressed out. It is an excellent food source for human and animal consumption.

Herbs de Provence: A French mixture of herbs consisting of thyme, rosemary, sage, marjoram, basil, and oregano.

Hijiki: A black seaweed that is usually sold dried and must be rehydrated. It is found at any local Asian market.

Hoisin: A Chinese sauce made from sugar, vinegar, soya bean, water, salt, wheat flour, garlic, sesame seeds, chili, and spices.

Hotel Pan: A rectangular metal pan that comes in any of a number of sizes and has a lip that allows it to sit in a storage shelf or steam table.

Huacatay: A Peruvian spicy mint that is quite difficult to find in the States. Mint or chilies can be used as substitutes in recipes.

Ice Bath: A large bowl of cold water filled with ice cubes in which to place vegetables after blanching or boiling them in order to stop the vegetables from cooking any further and to bring out their color.

Infusion: The liquid that remains after steeping an aromatic item in liquid to extract its flavor.

Julienne: Long thin-strip cut referring to vegetables.

Ketcup Manis: Made from soybeans, this intensely dark brown, syrupy thick Indonesian sauce is similar to soy sauce, but has a sweeter, more complex flavor. It is sweetened with palm sugar and is used widely in Indonesian cooking. Found at most Asian markets.

Korean Red Pepper Sauce: A hot garlic chili base sauce that is found in any Asian (and most chain) markets.

Lemon Grass: One of the most important flavorings in Thai and Vietnamese cooking. This herb has long, thin, gray-green leaves and a woody scallion-like base. Citral, an essential oil also found in lemon peel, gives lemon grass its sour lemon flavor and fragrance. It is available fresh or dried at most Asian markets. Lemon grass is also called citronella root and sereb.

Lime Leaves: The leaves of the kefir lime tree. The leaves are used similarly to bay leaves in stews, soups, and sauces. Found at your local Asian markets.

Lychee Fruit: The nutlike fruit of the lychee tree are 1 to 2 inches in diameter and covered by a thin, rough shell. The flesh is translucent and pearly white, extremely fragrant and juicy, crisp and sweet.

Madras Curry: An Indian curry powder that is blended from many different spices, including allspice, cloves, coriander seeds, cardamom seeds, cinnamon, and star anise.

Mandolin: A slicing device made from stainless steel with carbon blades. The blades can be adjusted to different cuts and thicknesses.

Milling: The process by which grain is ground into flour or meal.

Mince: To cut into tiny pieces (smaller than a dice).

Mirin: Sweet cooking rice wine found at any local Asian market.

Miso: A salty, occasionally sweetened, fermented paste made from soybeans and grains.

Mole Base: The concentrated base sauce used for making mole found at any local Mexican market.

Nam Pla Fish Sauce: A salty Indonesian fish sauce found at specialty Asian markets.

Panko Bread Crumbs: A particularly large Asian bread crumb found at any local Asian market.

Parchment: Heat-resistant paper used to line baking pans so that ingredients do not stick.

Parcook: To partially cook an item before storing or finishing by another method. Blanching is often parcooking.

Pesto: A thick puree of a mixture of fresh herbs—traditionally basil, oil, garlic, parmesan, and pine nuts. Pesto is best as a pasta sauce or soup garnish.

Phyllo Dough: A very thin Middle Eastern pastry dough used to make baklava, spinach spanakopita, and other sweet or savory dishes. It is found at most grocery stores in the frozen food section.

Rambutan: A small fruit with a crimson, orange, yellow, or green rind. Inside it has a single seed, which is surrounded by a translucent, grapelike flesh. Remove the flesh from the seed; it has a sweet, delicate flavor, which is similar, though a little more acidic, to the lychee.

Raw cane sugar: Sugar, after it is extracted from the sugar cane and dried. In its raw state, it is unbleached and unrefined.

Reduce: A term for decreasing the volume of a liquid by simmering or boiling.

Reduction: The product that results when a liquid is reduced.

Rehydration: Referring to dried fruits and vegetables, the process of covering the dried fruit or vegetable you wish to rehydrate with warm water and allowing it to sit for at least 30 minutes. It should double in size and be soft and edible.

Rendered Duck Fat: The fat that is left over after cooking a whole duck. This is used in French cooking for duck confit.

Rose Water: Made by boiling a gallon of water and pouring it over the petals from six roses. Cover the steeping water with plastic wrap until it cools. Strain the rose petals and use the water for certain recipes.

Serrano Chile: A Mexican chili that ranges from moderately spicy to hot and is found dried at Mexican markets.

Seitan: A meat substitute made from pressed wheat gluten. It is available at natural health food markets.

Shiro Miso Paste: A brownish red colored fermented bean paste native to Japan.

Shiso: Aromatic green jagged-edged leaf from the mint and basil family. It is used in salads, sushi, and sashimi, as well as a garnish. Green shiso is available from summer to fall in most Asian markets.

Soufflé Tin: Use a sweetened condensed milk tin, cleaned out and filed down on the inside so as not to cut your fingers. This proves to be an excellent tin for an individual soufflé and is a lot cheaper than buying them.

Spätzle Maker: A metal grater with large holes. The dough is forced through the holes with a spatula into the boiling water, forming worm-like noodles.

Spider: A flat, square strainer with a long handle. Used to fish out objects from hot oil or boiling water.

Spinning Mandolin: An Asian tool used to spin vegetables through several blades, making a spun spaghetti-like strand of vegetable. They are found at Asian markets and cooking stores.

Spring Roll Wrappers: Skins made from flour and egg that are used in Asian cuisine to make egg rolls and other items. They are found at any Asian market.

Tahini: A sauce made from sesame paste. This is a very popular condiment in Asia and in the Middle East, and is used to flavor sauces, main dishes, and desserts.

Tamari: A salty sauce made entirely from soybeans and found in most Asian markets.

Tamarind: This fruit of a tropical Asian evergreen tree is eaten fresh or used in the preparation of chutneys and curries. The reddish brown pods contain shiny dark seeds and are surrounded by a dense pulp, which is bittersweet and highly acidic.

Tepid Water: A term referring to luke-warm water.

Thai Curry Paste: A paste made from various spices, oil, garlic, and onions and found at your local Asian market.

Thai Chili: Small red or green chilies that are very hot and are used widely in Thai cuisine. They are found at your local Asian market in the frozen food section.

Toasted Hempnuts: Hempnuts toasted golden brown by dry-frying them in a heated iron skillet.

Udon Noodles: Wide noodles that are made from wheat flour and water. They are commonly used in Japanese cuisine and are found frozen or dried at your local Asian market.

Vegetable Stock: A broth made from root vegetables, spices, and water.

Vidalia Onions: A very light yellow onion native to southern Spain. They are sweet in taste and are found at most supermarkets.

Benjamin Franklin started one of America's first Papermills with Hemp Paper.

Benjamin Franklin started one of America's first paper mills with cannabis hemp. This allowed America to have a free colonial press without having to beg or justify the need for paper and books from England.

Resources

Organic Hemp Oil
P.O. Box 5773
Billericay
Essex, CM12 9YU
UK
(127) 765 78 92
chris@hempoil.co.uk
http://www.hempoil.co.uk

Sellers of organic hemp oil, nature's most powerful oil. There are ZERO known side effects. It's 100% safe and ensures maximum ERA effectiveness. This site recommends hemp oil for arthritis, ageing, acne, strong nails and hair, PMS, and general well being.

NaturART
Rinaldo Eckmann
Veltur 8
Sevelen, 9475
Switzerland
(81) 740 15 12
(81) 740 15 10
headoffice@naturart.com
www.naturart.com

Makers from Hempdrinks', C'apple', C'Cider', and CannaICE'. NaturART has been the leading hempseed food product developers in Europe since 1995!

Makers of Hulled Hempnuts, Hempnutoil, Hempnutflour, Hempmuelsi, Hemp-bars, and more. New products include Hemp Chocolate and Hemp Biscuits.

Spirit of Hanf
Günter Gsöls
Iglaseeg. 72
A-1190, Vienna
Austria
(431) 320 57 58
(431) 320 57 50
info@spirit-of-hanf.com
www.spirit-of-hanf.com

Worldwide widest selection of hemp drinks, including lemonade, beers, energy drinks, liquors, wines, schnaps, and syrup. Other products include hempseed oil, hemp massage oil, and hemp cosmetics. All products are registered trade-marks of Spirit of Hanf.

Fresh Hemp Foods Ltd.
Mike Fata
Box 2311
Winnipeg, Manitoba R3C 4A6
Canada
(204) 942-1185
(204) 956-5984
mike@hemperor.com
www.hemperor.com

All Manitoba Harvest Hemp Foods & Oils are grown without herbicides or pesticides, using non-genetically modified, "original source" hemp seeds. No additives or preservatives are used and all products are gluten-free. Products include Hemp Seed Oil, Hemp Seed Nut, Hemp Seed Nut Butter, and Hemp Seed Flour.

Galaxy Global Eatery
Denis Cicero
15 Irving Place
New York, NY 10003
(212) 777-3631
(212) 777-3224
denis@hempnut.com
www.galaxyglobaleatery.com

The innovative Galaxy Global Eatery, whose recipes are the essence of this cookbook, pioneers distinctive food ingredients and presentations all priced under US$10.00. Introducing galaxy hempnuts, private labeled oil, hempseeds, ice cream, and candy. Private labeled hemp coffee include Galaxy Hemp Vanilla, Galaxy Sumatra, Galaxy Costa Rican House Blend, and Galaxy Decaf. Galaxy's Hempnut Bar is packed with hempnuts and special ingredients.

Hempseed Oil Canada Inc.
Shaun Crew
P.O. Box 188
Ste. Agathe, Manitoba, R0G 1Y0
Canada
(204) 771-5008
(204) 882-2424
hempoilcan@techplus.com
www.hempoilcan.com

HOCI is dedicated to the procurement, processing, marketing, and distribution of bulk hemp seed, hempseed oil, roasted hempseed, hempnuts, sterilized hempseed, and seed cake to local, national, and international markets. They provide all export paperwork, certificate of sterilization, germination testing, THC, compositional analysis, and custom clearance. Products include Hempseed, Hemp Oil, Hempnuts, Roasted Seed, Sterilized Seed, and Seed Cake.

Mother Earth Enterprises, LLC
Denis Cicero
15 Irving Place
New York, NY 10003
(212) 777-3806
(212) 614-8132
denis@hempnut.com
www.hempnut.com

Mother Earth Enterprises promotes the sale of freshly hulled hempnuts from Canada and Eastern Europe and develops recipes for commercial applications in the food industry. Look for recipes on their website, www.hempnut.com, as well as wholesale and retail options. Products include wholesale hempnuts, hempseed oil, and hempseed, organic and conventional.

 Hempseed was part of the cargo on the Mayflower.

Nutiva
John Roulac
P.O. Box 1716
Sebastopol, CA 95472
(707) 823-2800
(707) 823-2424
info@nutiva.com
www.nutiva.com

Nutiva currently offers delicious-tasting Nutiva bars made with sunflower seeds, honey, shelled hempseeds, flax seeds, and pumpkin seeds. The shelled hempseeds are a rich source of minerals, vitamin E, complete protein, EFAs, and gamma linoleic acid (GLA). Products include hemp bars, snacks, confections, hulled hempnuts, and hempseed, shelled or toasted.

World Hemp
Chtistos & Victor
P.O. Box 309
Kapaa, HI 96746
(808) 823-HEMP
(808) 823-4367
info@worldhemp.com
www.worldhemp.com

Producers and sellers of hempseed oil and hempnuts.

HEMPOLA™
5-3405 American Drive
Mississauga, Ontario L4V 1T6
Canada
(800) 240-9215
(905) 678-6036
hempola@hempola.com
www.hempola.com

Hempola Valley Farms farm store offers a wide variety of hemp products from shoes to salad dressings. Other products include hemp oil, hemp flour, and body care products.

Herbal Products & Development
Paul Gaylon
PO Box 1084
Aptos, CA 95001
(831) 688-8706
(831) 688-8711
herbalproducts@pacifichemp.com

HP&D offers nutritional whole food concentrates and a variety of nutritional supplements, including organic virgin first-pressed non-sterilized hempseed oil and other products that have a hempseed oil base. They also offer a private label for high-grade hemp cosmetics.

King Hemp Trading Company
Sunny (Li Hui) SUNNY(LI HUI)
21 Dong Cang Men 1-4-1
XIAN
Shaanix, 710001
China
(86) 29 744 4951
(86) 29 742 2028
pacifichemp2000@yahoo.com

King Hemp Trading Company uses the hempseed from the Silk Road Area where farmers still grow organically. They cold press the live seeds and use the nitrogen methods to keep the oil production completely air tight. Products include hemp oil, hemp meal, and hempseed.

La Chanvriere de L'aube—LCDA
JB Le Texier
Rue de Gaulle
Bar s Aube
Aube,10200
France
(33) 325 27 3548
chanvriere@marisy.fr
www.marisy.fr/chanvriere

LCDA is a French hemp cooperative unit created in 1973. It gathers from 400 co-ops and more than 18,000 acres. A complete and carefully studied process has been set up to enhance hempseed values. They offer fine production of hemp seed, hemp cake, and cold pressed hemp oil. Wholesale only. "One foot in the soil, one foot in Industry."

Maple Ridge Farms Inc.
Martin Gareau
RR #3 Site#6 Compartment#4
Prince Albert, Saskatchewan S6V-5R1
Canada
(306) 922-8056
(306) 922-6189
mapleridge@sk.sympatico.ca

Processor of Hemp Essential Oil. Their oil has proven to be 1ppm, or non-detectable THC.

Spectrum Naturals
133 Copeland Street
Petaluma, CA 94952
(707) 778-8900
(707) 765-1026
spectrumnaturals@netdex.com
www.spectrumc.com

Producers and sellers of hempseed oil.

Suzy's Prairie Sun Canadian Hemp Products
Suzy Hamilton
P.O. Box 843
Nelson, BC V1L 6A5
Canada
(250) 825-9372
(250) 354-4615
kbarter@netidea.com

Producer and seller of hemp oil, hemp seed, hemp meal, and hemp-based cosmetics.

Boulder Hemp Company
Kathleen Chippi
P.O. Box 1794
Nederland, CO 80466
(303) 938-0195
bhc@hempfoods.com
www.hempfoods.com

Specializes in fine hemp foods. Hempseed is the most nutritionally complete grain on the planet. Products include hemp oil, hemp flour, and other hemp-based foods.

Gen-X Research Inc.
Sasha Przytyk
1237 Albert St.
Regina, Saskatchewan J0B 1C0
Canada
(306) 525-6519
(306) 569-5938
genx@net1fx.com
sasha@gen-xresearch.com
www.gen-xresearch.com

Producers and seller of hempseed.

Atlas Corporation
4712 Admiralty Way, Suite #233
Marina del Rey, CA 90292
(310) 838-9998
(310) 838-9995
atlas@atlascor.com
www.atlascor.com

Producers and sellers of hemp oil (large quantities).

Deer Garden Rejuvenative Foods
P.O. Box 8464
Santa Cruz, CA 95061
(800) 805-7957
www. rejuvenative.com

Producers of nut butters.

R&D Hemp
Box 73, Station P
Toronto, Ontario
Canada M5S 256
(416) 588-4209
www.ruthsfoods.ca

Products include hemp tortilla chips, hemp bars, hemp oil (large quantities), hemp wraps, hemp pasta, salad dressings, and more.

The Ohio Hempery
Guysville, Ohio
(800) BUY-HEMP
hempery@hempery.com
www.hempery.com

Products include hempseed, hemp oil, and body care products.

Hanf Dampf
D-73269 Hochdorf
Esslingen, Germany
(71) 53 95 08 52
(71) 53 95 08 53

Products include hempseed, hempnuts, hemp pressed cake, winnowed hemp coats, hempseed oil, hemp mead.

CannaBioland
Armin Kaser
Litzistorf
3178, Bosingen
Switzerland
(26) 497-9610
(26) 497-9611
Email: info@cannabioland

Products include hempseed oil, hempseed, hemp beer, hemp jam, and hemp pasta.

Vermont Hemp Company
P.O. Box 5233
Burlington, VT 05402
(802) 865-2646
(888) 266-HEMP
Email: hempydog@hempseed.com

Products include hemp ice cream, hemp flour, and hemp oil.

NOWAKORN
Franz Sieghl
Managing Director
Heidenreichstein
Reg. Gen. M.b.h.
3860 Heidenreichstein N.O.
Austria
(28) 625-2325

NOWAKORN is an original dehuller of hempnuts. Products include biological hempseed, hempnuts, and hempseed oil.

Index

Hemp Sambal Mentah, 74

Hemp Speckknodel, 131

Hemp Sweet Potato-Quinoa Soufflé, 110

Hemp Tofu Corndogs, 107

Hemp Tortillas, 150

Hemp Waffles, 16

Hempesto, 164

Hempizza Dough, 145

Hempnut Almond Baklava, 258

Hempnut Bison Tamale, 208, 210

Hempnut Black Rice Cakes, 199

Hempnut Bread Twists, 221–22

Hempnut Caesar Dressing, 69

Hempnut Cashew-Cilantro Pesto, 79

Hempnut Chestnut Gnocchi, 174

Hempnut Chickpea Crêpes, 18–19

Hempnut Chocolate Truffles, 260

Hempnut Chocolatissimo, 259

Hempnut Cookies, 245

Hempnut Cranberry-Quinoa Muffins, 244

Hempnut-Crusted Catfish Filets, 189

Hempnut-Crusted Goat Cheese Salad, 53–54

Hempnut-Crusted Lamb Chops, 203–5

Hempnut-Crusted Stuffed Hearts of Palm, 148–49

Hempnut-Crusted Tofu Steak, 152, 154

Hempnut Fried Chicken, 213

Hempnut Hummus, 109

Hempnut Johnny Cakes, 126

Hempnut Lentil Stew with Speckknodel, 130

Hempnut Mushroom Cakes, 90–91

Hempnut Mushroom Ravioli with Beet & Fennel Garnish, 168–69

Hempnut Pita, 231

Hempnut Pumpkin Preserve, 13

Hempnut Ravioli with Shiitake Mushroom, Kale, & Broccolini Filling, 167

Hempnut Romesco Sauce, 120

Hempnut Sage Buttermilk Biscuits, 243

Hempnut Spätzle with Roasted Vegetables, 176–77

Hempnut Tahini, 160

Hempnut Watercress-Avocado Dressing, 68

Hempnut Whipped Cream, 6, 262

Hempnut Yucca Fritters with Mushroom & Herb Stuffing, 113–14

Hempnuts, xxv–xxvi
    cooking with, xxvi
    nutrition and, xxvi

HEMPOLA, 289

Hempseed, xix–xxi
    nutrition and, xx, 161
    toasting, xxi
    washing, xxi

Hempseed oil, xxii, xxiv
    cooking with, xxiv
    infused, 82–84
    nutrition and, xxii, xxiv, 75
    other oils vs., xxii
    storing, xxiv
    uses for, 78, 187, 194, 207, 233

Hempseed Oil Canada Inc., 287

Herbal Products & Development, 289–90

Herodotus, 207

Hoisin Tofu Crème Anglaise, 19

Honeydew melon
    Gingered Melon Hempade, 34
    Minted Melon Norimaki, 102–3

Hot dogs
    Hemp Tofu Corndogs, 107